WHAT DID YOU DO IN THE COLD WAR, DADDY?

-from Kilroy up to and beyond Elvis an unbroken line of American G.I.s spent a piece of their youth on Freedom's First Line of Defense

JACK TARVIN & ED PAQUETTE

Photo Credits

Front Cover
Cowden, Dave. "Watchtower/on Czech Border." 1967. jpg

Back Cover
Paquette, Ed. "Gatehouse Monument/authors at Pond Barracks."
2007. jpg

ISBN: 1500719897
ISBN 13: 9781500719890
Library of Congress Control Number: 2014913935
CreateSpace Independent Publishing Platform
North Charleston, South Carolina

for
all the G.I.s who served
on Freedom's First Line
of Defense in the Cold War

ACKNOWLEDGEMENTS

WE WOULD LIKE to acknowledge the many kindnesses and excellent assistance we have received over the period this book was only a work in progress.

Our sincere thanks to June Prince who combed through our text, found our mistakes, and helped us make something out of our efforts. Thanks, June for making us look like we know something. We would never think of doing another without your help.

And, many special thanks to our comrades in arms out there on the Pond immersed in a Cold War and a marvelous adventure all at once, especially Joe & Peggy Cournoyer, Dave Cowden, Marty Freedman, Jay Halpern, Michael & Ann Noftsger, Merlin Seibold, Jacinto Saucedo, Roy Pirrung, Olin & Sally Wenrick, Thomas Westgate. Our story would not be complete without recognizing our fond memories of the late Gail Pirrung, and Pete Taylor who we may have lost, but have not forgotten. We also thank our readers and especially we would like to thank our brides, Pat Paquette, and Betty York for bearing the burden of our singular focus and ignoring our many faults.

Thanks, Ed & Jack

PROLOGUE

Out on Post 29-Camp Rötz-Czechoslovakian Border-Christmas, 1968

In the Moon of the Long Night, I see my silent breath. Tall evergreens stand still on a blanket of snow. The long jagged scar of the Iron Curtain cuts a path through the Oberpfalz. Up in the Czech towers blackened silhouettes peer at me through their dark eyes.

I walk, I watch, I listen. I hear footsteps on a cushion of new snow, my own I think. I feel my enemy in the shadows close by crouched low in the sting of minus six degrees Celsius. Inside this cold night every little breeze tingles through me, sucks any cozy warmth out from under me.

In an unlikely chorus, a toasty brown hare and my heart leap up in front of me, and as a little shout of distress escapes my frozen lungs, the hare and my heart race away together looking for safety.

My awkward shout wakes up the searchlights inside the Czech towers, they pop on, flare up one by one. Radiant beams of light sweep the wire. The bright glare washes out the landscape. Loudspeaker commands are given in Czech, in German, in Polish, in some other tongue. A beam of light swings toward me,

I step back into the shadows, the brilliant ray passes over me. Then, the light fades, as each light dies off in a random sequence.

I keep pace with this silent night and blindly slip through the darkness into Post 29's deepest corners. I only double back when I can see again.

After and hour, I claim the cold as my only companion. The snow clouds slip into place above us, it comes down heavy, again. Big wet flakes accumulate in deep piles off to my right, my ledt, ahead, behind. Even in my Mickey Mouse boots and my high stride, I still stumble, fall, get up again, find my weapon, move on.

Now I wait for it, listen, cringe in the anticipation of the awful sound it makes. Then, I think maybe not tonight, maybe not this time. Hidden in the deep, the dead load of it presses down, and the weight of this new fallen snow triggers a Czech land mine across the curtain. The smell of cordite, the concussive blast finds me, pushes me into my companion's white blanket of cold. Clouds of snow, clods of dirt rumble through the forest, loose pieces of shrapnel spin through time.

I wait, I listen, I wait to listen. In the pinkish glow of dawn, I hear the struggle of big green engines crawling toward me, plowing their way through this bitter night just to bring me home, and leave another me out here to walk Post 29.

1

ON THE POND

WE SPENT DAYS and days, and as many nights getting here in the complete suspense of a raw recruit, while in the most wretched state of being there is in the United States Armed Forces, as an 'In Transit' soldier/sailor/ marine [sleepless nights, rumpled clothing, locked inside the confines of a plane, a building, a truck, a train], on our way to who knows where, and for most of us, on our own for the first time in our lives on a strange and exotic mission, and not a single one of us knew exactly what we were doing.

We kept straining get a peek of this place called Germany, from thirty thousand feet above, from the window of a train, from the back of a Deuce and Half [a two and a half ton truck]. And, sometimes, we get a little peek at things we've never seen before, at tall pines with branches only in the top quarter of the trees, a starkly modern architecture replaces bombed out sections of cities with only a few of the ancient structures stuck in between, people in uniform who look like generals turn out to be postmen, cryptic traffic signs that don't make any sense, but we kept going around from this place to the other with a few sidewinding detours just like we knew what we were doing.

We went from our homes at the end of our leave to Fort Dix, New Jersey, to New York JFK or Wrightstown Air Force Base, to Rhein Mein Air Force Base, to the 21st Replacement Battalion in Frankfurt, to the 2nd Armored Cavalry Regimental Headquarters in Nurnberg, and finally to Amberg.

We kept looking for Nazis, and occasionally we found one. Sometimes in an obvious drunken state of denial and anger, screaming out his angst at the thought of our presence here. But, more often we saw them in a more subtle, self possessed way that veils their deeply suppressed hate, fanaticism and longing for another lost time.

Most of our travel was at night, so we couldn't see much, and mostly alone so we had to find our own way in a foreign place, in a foreign language, in our best naïveté. If we had not been so young and so wide eyed, we probably would have wondered what might happen to us next, but we had no idea which way was up, so we just kept on going until we got here.

Sitting on the cold January steps of the Bahnhof in Nurnberg, a young recruit waits for a transport to Merrell Barracks. As he waits an old inebriated Sergeant stumbles up the stairs and takes a long hard look at the young man.

"Whererere ya hea, head, headed, Trooper?"

The young man glances down at the note in his hand, "Looks like a place called Amberg, I guess."

The old Sergeant laughs, slaps the kid on the back and says, "HA, ev-ever-everybody oughta to ha-hav to ser-serve a tour of du-duty th-there."

The young man manages to get out a, "Huh?"

"See ya fer-fer yoself, gu-gu-good luck, Trooper."

Things like this could make us wonder about some of the choices we've made, but it's too late for that now.

So, we find out that our post, our unit, the 3d Reconnaissance Squadron of the 2d Armored Cavalry is in Amberg, Germany near the Czech border, and that this place is stuck in something called the Oberpfalz. The Oberpfalz is mostly rural pieces of history hidden inside the biggest forest in Germany, spread out over hills, mountains, shallow valleys, and deep inside these woods are castles, walled medieval fortress towns, and small villages.

The city elite, the ones from Frankfurt, or Berlin call these small towns Kuh Dorfs [Cowtowns], or sometimes, if they are really mean spirited, the German Kongo which might be the American equivalent of a New Yorker's disdain for Appalachia, or something like that. This is an ancient place, a place way out in the countryside that even feels old and primal like no place else we've ever seen. Even the dirt looks old.

When we finally get to our post near Amberg, we find ourselves on a hundred acres or so of hilltop above the Kaiser Wilhelm Ring [a street] that encircles the medieval town of Amberg]. This place is called Pond

Barracks, formerly, the Mohl Kaserne of the Third Reich, a Nazi outpost. We cannot seem to get away from the past, the history our fathers made here, or the ancient history of this place.

This unit is characterized by two words in its designated name, 'Reconnaissance', and 'Cavalry'. Recon, meaning the scouts out in front of the pack and Cavalry, meaning we're mounted and mobile, which can be a scary thing with all these kids out there armed, mobile and believing they're invincible. And, the cavalry is still the cavalry, which means everyone, no matter what they actually do day to day as far as work goes, has a primary combat MOS [military occupational specialty] first. Not every personnel office in the Army needs a .50 caliber machine gun, and an armored personnel carrier, unless they're Recon & Cavalry.

On the surface we are in disguise, the Pond looks sort of collegiate; at the core there is a huge quadrangle with a parade field at the center [covered in small gray rocks [no mowing is my guess]. The quad is surrounded by 2 to 3 story tan stucco buildings each with a red clay tile roof that glows bright in the sunshine, and in the gray daylight of winter, the colors deepen into a richer value that hides any flaws.

On the corners of the parade field there are Poplar trees, in straight rows of four each, at each corner of the field. It's kind of an accidental academic setting which veils the threat that lies beneath.

The only thing that looks out of place here is in between How [Howitzer] Battery and K Troop on an elevated platform there sets this vintage World War II

M26 Pershing Tank, a solitary survivor of war which betrays our true identity. This M26 is occasionally used to fire a single [powder only] round between the playing of 'Retreat' and 'To The Colors' each afternoon. It just squats there alone like its just brooding over our next move.

The flagstaff, between the Headquarters Building and the Headquarters Troop barracks, is opposite the Pershing Tank. At one end of the parade field there is a Helipad in front of the Mess Hall.

On this end, the Consolidated Mess Hall with its onion dome and clock looks sort of Russian like. The Mess sits opposite the S-4/EM Club. And, along both sides of the parade field these same stucco buildings, Headquarters & I Troop, HQ's Troop, Howitzer Battery/M Company, K Troop, L Troop, and the Missile Battery all flanking the parade field make up the quad, the Dispensary/BOQ [Bachelor Officer's Quarters] are set behind the Mess Hall.

Behind the HQ's Troop Barracks are the wash racks and the Motor Stables; this makes for an interesting view just across from our rooms, and a noxious aroma, [tanks, trucks, self-propelled howitzers, and diesel fumes]. From there, the Motor Stables [a Motor Pool in the cavalry's nostalgic imagination] flows back to the very rear of the kaserne, and all the stables [the garages] are surrounded by armored personnel carriers, trucks, jeeps, tanks, self propelled Howitzers, VTRs [Vehicle, Tank Recovery], and such, which are parked all over the place. Up on a raised plateau way back there in the rear, there is open piece of ground that they call an athletic field, this is a major stretch of the imagination.

Behind How Battery, there are several low slung buildings, the Officers Club, the NCO Club, the USO Club, the Photo Lab, the Laundromat, and for some strange reason there are tennis courts back there [we never see anyone play tennis here].

The Chapel, the Snack Bar, the Bowling Alley [two lanes], the movie theater, the library, and the power plant are over behind the K & L Troop buildings. There is a substantial stucco wall around most of this place, except way back in the Motor Stables area it becomes just a fence.

The dependent housing area for the families of officers and senior Non-commissioned Officers is off post outside the perimeter wall opposite the USO Club and the Photo Lab. The airfield and ammo dump are also off post just a couple of Klicks [a kilometer] out from the Pond.

The door knobs are levers, the windows open like double cabinets, the roads are cobblestone, everyone you see is wearing O.D. green [our pickle costumes] or khaki, except on weekends. Most everyone here is young, every day is a new day, and we never notice any of our mortal flaws, we only notice how good we look, and how wonderful it is to be here in this strange new world where the only objective [besides being Freedom's First Line of Defense] is to have a good time, where we get four Deutsche Marks to the dollar, and we get to see a piece of the world in a way we would never ever see it if we weren't American G.I.s in Europe.

On the Pond there are secrets, too, military secrets, and hidden places that are tucked away out of sight. Hidden in underground bunkers there are tactical nuclear weapons that can be launched by the Missile Battery, or from a self propelled Howitzer. Behind the altar in the chapel covered by a heavy drape there is a doorway through the perimeter wall to the outside [this comes in handy sometimes]. In the basement of the Headquarters Building there is a PAL-CRYPTO machine [a encryption device for sending/receiving coded messages] hidden behind two steel doors with a bulletproof peephole that has a steel cover that slides open/closed from the inside by the armed personnel on the door, and inside the message center. Underneath the parade field there is an abandoned Wehrmacht [Nazi] Motor Pool. Out in our Motor Stables there is a pile of new periscope covers discarded from M60 Tanks as soon as they get here. In the basement of the Dispensary there is an escape tunnel that comes out in downtown Amberg. And, there are utility tunnels from the power plant to all of the other buildings [steam heat].

Now, the real story of the Cold War begins here. It may not be what you might think of as Freedom's First Line of Defense, but for every hour of our lives spent staring out there into the Iron Curtain, there were another hundred hours of ordinary Army routines, a few fleeting bouts of hysterical laughter, and a couple of sensational moments of absolute terror that filled our days and nights.

An ordinary day on the Pond goes something like this, well; actually it goes exactly like this. Reveille is at 0600 hours. One half of the personnel from the Personnel Office who live in Headquarters Troop, get up and go outside for the Reveille formation. We decided on this strategic reserve resource earlier on one cold morning in January when no one wanted to get out of bed much less go outside. This is an economy of scale; only half of us have to go out in the cold [no one is supposed to know this, so don't tell anyone]. The ones that have to get up, if it's their turn, don't bother to actually get dressed, they just put on a hat, field jacket, pants, and slip on their boots without bothering to lace them up, and go stand in the cold rain/ snow/sleet/ fog/dark long enough to get the flag up, then we go back inside and get back in bed for a few more minutes.

If you're wondering why that nowadays, we sometimes get up, shave and brush our teeth, then go and sit down and eat breakfast before we shower, here's why. After breakfast the shower room is less crowded than before breakfast. Then, we get dressed, straighten up our room, clean the shower room [a regular duty of the Personnel Section], and when it's time for us to fall out for the official Morning Formation, we go back outside for the real thing. This is where they actually count heads, and assign a crew for Repair & Utilities [more on this later].

After the morning formation, our section goes off behind the Headquarters Troop building for Police Call. We form a line, E-5s to the rear, and we go along the back of HQ Troop Barracks and pick up all the trash from the night before that was thrown out the windows of HQ Troop barracks, thrown out by, you guessed it, the very same people who are picking it all up the very next morning. I don't know why this is, it just is.

From here, we [the Remington Raiders, after the manual typewriter of the same name], that's us, go to the office. The first order of business is to take the Bratwurst Run order from the people in the Headquarters building, this order is usually somewhere in the neighborhood of twenty to thirty bratwurst [a brat is a hard roll with a Nurnberger bratwurst inside the hard roll].

Then, someone who has a car races through the streets of downtown Amberg looking for a street vendor. I think they hide from us, because most people just stop by their cart and order a brat, we have to chase them down to fill our order of vierundzwanzig (24) brats. Sometimes, if it's a holiday, this is not an easy task. One such morning all we could find was a Curry Wurst vendor. Pete said, this would be okay, but it wasn't.

As the morning goes along we do what we do in Personnel. We complete the Morning Report (a report that says who is here, who is there, who is AWOL, who is in civilian custody [usually only one guy, the guy who robbed and shot a cab driver way back where in the forgotten past, is still in a German prison, we cut orders [Walter used to do this till he went nuts], we process people into the 3rd Herd, we process people out of the 3rd Herd, we promote our friends who are leaving, we update personnel records, we try to find slots for people where there are no slots on the T.O.&E. [Table of

Organization & Equipment], we drink coffee, we send new guys to How Battery to get the keys to the parade field, How Battery sends them over to S-4, S-4 sends them over to K Troop, K Troop sends them over to the Dispensary, and so on and on they go until the new guy figures it out or gives up and comes back to the office, but after doing this we all learn where everything is, or where it should be.

At lunch we go over to the Mess Hall or the Snack Bar, then after lunch we wander around the post aimlessly with our hands in our pockets, or at least that's what the C.O. keeps screaming about when he sees us aimlessly wandering about with our hands in our pockets after lunch.

Then, back at the office, it's more of the same until Mail Call, when one of us goes over to the HQ Troop Mail Room and picks up the real mail, and one of us gets the Regimental Mail package from the S-1 office across the hall. First, we read our personal mail, show everyone the pictures we get, if anyone gets a bennie box [a box from home with candy, snacks, cookies, and stuff] we share the wealth. Then, we get down to the regimental stuff, usually just mox nichts Army crap like where is our Morning Report from 3 April 1953, and stuff like that.

In the afternoon we try to avoid typing anything for our Personnel Officer, the last time Pete had to do this, he typed the same letter nine times before Dewey marked up the ninth copy and said, "Oh, I didn't mean to do that. Just type it up again and we'll send it out."

Pete couldn't do it, so Olin said to forget it, he'll never remember.

Okay, here's the squirrelly part, there are a few of us, no one will ever really admit to this, who secretly like to be outside when 'Retreat' and 'To The Colors' is playing. Retreat is a ceremony where they play a bugle call called 'Retreat', everyone stands at ease facing the flagstaff, then sometimes this is followed by a blast from the old Pershing Tank, then everyone outside comes to 'Attention', 'Present Arms' [which means salute] and they play 'To The Colors' as our flag comes down for the day. As we stand there, listening to these bugle calls, watching our flag being lowered for the day, it kind of tingles at the back of your neck and makes you smile for some reason. This is how it is on the Pond.

This place is named after Lieutenant Colonel Leroy "Fireball" Pond, KIA-1945, awarded the Distinguished Service Cross [DSC] [2], the Silver Star Medal [SSM], the Bronze Star Medal [BSM] [2], the Purple Heart Medal [PHM], the French Croix de Guerre with Silver Star.

2

THE PERSONALITY SHOP

WE DON'T KNOW who thought this up, but we all like it. Everyone calls our office, the Personality Shop instead of the Personnel Office. It makes sense, there are some real personalities locked up in here.

This group is like a rare slice of America, and we probably couldn't have done a better job of picking our friends if we had to do it ourselves. Basically, a cavalry trooper winds up in Personnel for one of two reasons. One, he can type, or two, he has some guardian spirit who watches over him because he can't be trusted to always do the right thing, or the safe thing all the time.

The best thing about the Army is the people. We all bring a little piece of our place, culture, background with us to Amberg, and each one is equipped with his own accent, experience, and unique perspective on America. We share all these strange customs, sounds, ideas, talents with each other. Here on the Pond we have a wonderful cross section of our country from one end to the other, with all kinds of weirdness, mannerisms, sayings, ideas, habits, surprising ways to say and do things that we've never dreamed of before, with a great range of new extreme pranks to try out on each other, and time is no barrier, we're all rich with bundles of hours, and days, and weeks and months of time with not much to do with it, but have fun.

While Personnel is a terrific job, it takes an extreme kind of discipline to do this work well, extreme because the possibility of succumbing to a fatal case of chronic boredom is always looming in the background. Just think about it, just think about this one example, DA Form 4, item 1, the date, day-month-year, a pencil entry, do you understand? How much of this stuff could you take?

As a permanent duty station, this place is one of the best. This is much different from being in a Basic Training Company, or an Advanced Training Company. Everyone becomes a human being again, and things are pretty relaxed. If you just do your job, and keep your nose clean, this place is a great place to be if you have to be in the military.

The only scary thing about being here is the ever present ominous past of this country that has kind of seeped into every deep dark depression in the landscape. If you want to, you don't have to go far from here to find a drunken Nazi, the solemn and awful remains of a concentration camp [estimates range from 5 to 7 thousand concentration camps in Nazi Germany], the remnant of some piece of destroyed military equipment, a crumbling concrete bunker, the modern interior of a bombed out building.

However, if you look just a little bit closer you'll smile, when you find the faded graffiti left behind by our fathers, 'Kilroy Was Here', or the much more recent notes left here by our older brothers, 'Elvis Was Here'.

If we ever wonder how we got here, it doesn't take long to figure this out either.

The other side of this same coin is just as amazing. The closer we get to the border, the better we get treated. Everyone, all over Europe, all over the world, knows this. It's just that the people up close to the Iron Curtain know it better than most, they know it every day, and they know it by the refugees who risk everything to crawl, climb, run, crash, dig, or get out of there any way they can. And, they know it from the bodies that hang up on the concertina wire and rot. And, they know it from the little miracles of the desperate few that make it beyond this barrier to freedom.

The people up here, the ones up close up to the wire, have a kind of respect and appreciation for us. The kind of respect and appreciation [that as kids] we've never known before, and this feels pretty good]. This makes it worth being here, and we're very proud of our place, and our duty here.

3

USAREUR ALERT

Tic..., Tic..., Tic... Tic..., Tic..., Tic... Tic. Tic. Tic. [pause] Shhhhhhh...Tic...Shhhhhh...Tic. Psssssssst.

Wet veins of steam heat slap at lazy valves, silly vapors sing through pressure points that whistle. Warm air condenses on cold window panes; the frosty shade of night is relentless, harsh.

Tic..., Tic..., Tic... Tic..., Tic..., Tic... Tic. Tic. Tic. [pause] Shhhhhhh...Tic...Shhhhhh...Tic. Psssssssst.

Four sovereign dreams swirl through the room, slip through filters designed by Dave or Pete, Jacinto or Tommy. By chance they switch places, swap perils. Loose pieces of sad and funny fall through the cracks, and dance down the wrong path, collide, shatter.

Tic..., Tic..., Tic... Tic..., Tic..., Tic... Tic. Tic. Tic. [pause] Shhhhhhh...Tic...Shhhhhh...Tic. Psssssssst.

The rhythm mimics time, mocks the long night. The mindless tempo disrupts a drowsy breath, steals a reckless heartbeat, and yet gives balance inside the dark unknown. Without notice, it stops. It curls up into a new key, restarts the beat in an erratic fashion that wakes even the dead. In this whole great night, we listen for the slightest fault in the endless tones of each solemn moment.

In a dim closet down the hall, the CQ [Charge of Quarters] hooks up the battery powered Alert Siren. Waves of whining screams penetrate the weary hours; groans interrupt vile curses in the cold climate of anticipation. Some joker on the second floor picks up a bugle, blows 'Boots and Saddles'. The NEO Team picks up where it left off last night looking for the exits.

Dave didn't know what he was getting into. No one thinks of all the practical aspects hidden right here in plain sight. He thought he had it made until someone told him to get over to S-4 and draw his TA 50-901. He didn't have a clue; he had to look up that one. It sounds like something other than what it is, but as it turns out, there is this one simple, obvious truth, it's not just cold here, it's very cold. This really is a Cold War, and your TA 50-901 is your Cold Weather Gear [Parkas, liners, layers and layers, 'Mickey Mouse' boots with tire valves on the side that you air up after you get them on]. There is no excuse for frost bite, in fact, it is punishable by an Article 15 [non-judicial punishment], damaging government property.

Down in the armory, weapons fly through the air in cadence with a rhyming pattern of names and numbers. Sleepy stares come into focus when butts and stocks slap empty palms. The rattle of ammo belts, full magazines, the clicks and clacks of ordnance in motion creeps along in a steady pace of its own.

Out in the motor stables, Tommy slips through the driver's hatch of an M-114 APC [Armored Personnel Carrier], puts his helmet on backwards, which puts his mic keys on opposite sides of his chest from where they are supposed to be, he clicks the wrong button, goes out on the net, "Man, this is all f#$%ed up and so am I."

The XO, Major Smith, clicks in, "Black Knight 5… this is Black Knight 5. Okay, who said that? IDENTIFY. IDENTIFY YOURSELF. Over."

Tommy squenches up his face. He's confused, maybe not yet sober enough to make sense of the critical details of speech. He gets an idea, and reaches up feels around for his head, finds it, he straightens up his headgear, decides he has his helmet on backwards, and clicks out to the net once again, "Hey, man. I may be f%&%ed up, but I ain't that f#$%ed up!. Out."

Everyone who can keys his mic at the same time. The static over the radio, and the laughter from the peanut gallery veil the curses of the XO. He doesn't try again.

Pete wrestles a stack of duffle bags into the track, one of them is way too light. Which means, someone, someone like Jay, had the good sense to bring us snacks and candy bars, instead of his cold weather gear, to this party.

Tracks, trucks, jeeps, tanks, howitzers, and VTRs crank up into a cacophony that swells up in stages of low rumbles to mellow grumbles, to a consistent roar, to a deafening disharmony that overwhelms the night in a thunder of sound. The noises, odors, the vile taste of diesel foul up the atmosphere. The bitter cold bites back.

Now, eleven hundred and fifty boys, the most irresponsible carefree people in the world, armed with every conceivable weapon of war from Pete's war tomahawk to tactical nuclear weapons, warm up to the cold night, and head out for the Czech border.

A column of armored vehicles squeezes through the main gate, where Eddy stands and counts as he touches the cold hard skin of each one with his little stick of chalk. None of us know why he does this.

The NEO Team's single track, the 114, and our creepy jeepy, salvaged from the discard pile, pull up behind Eddy's VW bug outside the main gate, and we watch the 3rd Herd roll off into the night. While we wait for our fearless leader, Sergeant First Class George Tyler, everyone gets out of the jeep, and walks up the street. The damn thing still stinks so bad we can't just sit there in it.

We got the creepy jeepy because no one else wants to use it. The last one to use it was Specialist Carmody. Specialist Carmody turned the creepy jeepy over on top of himself and PFC Morton. At first, we couldn't find them, and they were carried as AWOL on the Morning Report for sixteen days until we did find them, but we were way too late.

None of us even considered the possibility of getting ourselves killed over here. We used to think we were part of a grand scheme of invincibility and reckless abandon, but there is no speed limit on the Autobahn, no way to outrun an unexpected explosion, no way to keep from drowning in your own puke if your too drunk to turn over, and there are no roll bars on jeeps. We are nineteen, maybe twenty. Oh, there are some old folks, Olin is twenty-six, and we count on him to tell us when we're over the line. There were eleven of us who didn't listen to the warnings they were given, the rest of us are just lucky.

We packed up Carmody's and Morton's personal stuff [a function of the Personnel Office], and sent it to their folks in Kentucky and Oregon. We put a letter in each box, we all signed the letters, I'm certain this didn't help much.

Sergeant Tyler pulls up next to the track in his '58 Ford Thunderbird. He grins, guns the engine a little, the rumble of his California Glass Packs vibrate off the perimeter wall of the Pond. Our fathers left here twenty-three years ago, and for some strange reason or other we'll put our own sons up here twenty-three years from now.

He calls out to Tommy, "Okay, Hot Shot, park that hunk of scrap back up in the Motor Stables, and we'll wait here for ya." He kind of leans out the window and looks back to where we're standing near the creepy jeepy, he yells, "Issue them death notices, and meet us out at the airfield."

What Sergeant Tyler means is that The NEO Team, the Noncombatant Evacuation Order Team, that's us, should now proceed to its mission. Our mission is to round up all the noncombatants, the wives and children of the real soldiers, and lead them out of harm's way when the 250 divisions of Russians stationed along the

Iron Curtain invade Western Europe. Taking a more practical approach, what Sergeant Tyler really means is what he said, 'issue them death notices', which means to go tell everyone we're having an alert.

Dave, Pete and Jacinto pile in the creepy jeepy and we make our first run at the Dependent Housing Area to notify the wives and children of the officers and NCOs. An official notice is placed in each mailbox, "Good Morning. This morning USAREUR [the United States Army Europe] conducted a Readiness Test Alert. Had this been an actual alert you would have been instructed to follow the protocols defined in your Operation BUGOUT booklet. Thank you, The NEO Team."

When we get through the Dependent Housing Area it gets even more interesting. We try to catch up with Eddy and his group who are out there somewhere trying to find all the other quarters where dependents that live 'out there on the economy' somewhere are scattered out all over this nine-hundred thirty-two year old town.

When we get to any of our friend's places, we leave this alternative notice, "Good Morning. This morning USAREUR conducted a Readiness Test Alert. Had this been an actual alert you would, of course, be dead and would never see this note. Thank you, The NEO Team."

Out at the airfield, we all squeeze into the little guard hooch in the middle of the entrance road. A bottle of Golden Wedding Bourbon is passed around; a few of us take a swig, and regret it. There are enough

bodies in here now to warm up this small space, but it's getting hard to breathe. Jacinto and Pete go outside to get some cold oxygen in their lungs. When they get away from the guard hooch, a pinkish gray horizon peeks up over the tree line. Most alerts end like this, in another pinkish-gray dawn in the Oberpfalz.

4

REPAIR & UTILITIES

REPAIR & UTILITIES is the secret word for the Trash Detail. The Trash Detail consists of riding around in the back end of a 5 ton truck, and when we come to a stop, one of us jumps down, grabs a fifty-five gallon drum of trash and tosses it up onto the back of the truck, the other guy turns it upside down and shakes out the debris, and tosses it off the truck, the guy on the ground picks it up and puts in back in place and climbs back aboard the truck, and we go to the next stop.

The appeal of this duty is driven by one singular perk, [and, as it turns out, three other totally marvelous and nexpected ancillary perks].

Depending on how fast you can get this done [picking up all the trash on the entire post, driving out to the dump, and back ever how many times it takes], when you are finished, you get the rest of the day off. Don't laugh; this is back when a half a day off really meant something, regardless of what we may have smelled like.

This detail is assigned two to three mornings a week depending on the season while we are in the Morning Formation. First, they ask for volunteers. Of course, it is a physical law of the universe that no one ever volunteer for anything, so, this pretty much leaves it up to the big brain guys, Sergeant Willie Ray Dutton, or Sergeant Roy Gene Grumbles, or 'Spin & Marty' as we call them, to pick the Trash Detail Crew from the ranks.

This is where it gets hard, because 'Spin & Marty' look at this like it's a way to get even with some of us. But, to us this duty is a marvelous way to get some time off, so we can't let them know this. It would spoil the fun, and make it so it might be difficult to get yourself picked for the Trash Detail, if either of these two might think they were doing us a favor. So, just before it occurs to Spin or Marty that it's time to choose the crew for the Repair & Utilities Detail, everyone is trying to somehow piss them off, so we will be picked for the job.

One cautionary note, this is not the case in the wintertime. In the wintertime, the Trash Detail includes the removal of the coal ash cans from the power plant and this is back breaking work that requires a chain pulley to lift the coal ash cans, and it takes the whole day and sometimes into the evening. So, when the cold weather comes in, everyone is doing the exact opposite of what they are doing in the warmer weather, and acting completely different, [i.e., actually being nice to Spin & Marty] because no one wants to do this if it's cold. This, however, is extremely confusing for Spin and Marty because they notice this tremendous difference in how we are treating them depending on the weather, but they cannot, to save their souls, figure out exactly why this difference is weather related. They just wonder why everyone treats them so well, in the winter and no one likes them in the spring or summer.

Marty is the smart one, relative to Spin's level of smarts, and one day he gets a couple of us aside, and says, "I know what you guys are up to, and it isn't working." At first, we think maybe he knows, but as it turns out, he just thinks he knows, because the next thing he says is, "You can't expect to get any favors from me no matter how much you lay it on."

Two of the best Trash Detail Engineers in the 3rd Herd are, Roy & Jack. They both have a hidden talent for this challenging work, and they almost set the record time for the fastest Trash Detail Run in the known history of USAREUR. On a balmy, unseasonably warm, sunny and humid day in May of 1968, Roy & Jack were on track to make Trash Detail Run history, a record that might still stand today, if only.

It was on this very same day that Roy & Jack discovered the Sirens of the Oberpfalz, the Buschbohm Sisters, Adalwolfa, Adellinde, and Adellonda. Of course, they have no regrets, but they still wonder what it might have been like to be in the record books.

It was on the last run of the day, on the return trip from the Dump to the Pond that things went askew. Billy Wayne was driving the Trash truck, Roy & Jack were sitting in the back synchronizing their watches and anticipating their victory, when Billy Wayne just veers off the road, and cuts a wide ugly swath into a crop of Hops about halfway back from the Dump. When he finally realizes his error he slams on the brakes and Roy & Jack make an abrupt slide from the rear of the truck up to a place in back of the cab where they leave two similar shallow depressions.

When we pull ourselves together and climb down to check on Billy Wayne, he is out of the truck, and standing there in the Hops field looking back from where we had come. He has this lost and forlorn look on his face as he just stares into space, the sweat pouring off his brow, a silly stupid smile on his face and a twinkle in his eye.

Roy is yelling at him, "Hey, Hey, You, Stupid! What's the deal? What's wrong with you?" As he says this, the words just bounce off Billy Wayne, fall to the ground and sink into the plowed up Hops, and there is no response. Billy Wayne can't hear him, he just stands there, he can't move. He tries to mumble something, but it's unintelligible.

Roy keeps questioning him, and Jack tries to figure out what Billy is staring at. He follows his gaze to a little cottage a few yards back and he studies the little shack and the surroundings, then he sees what Billy Wayne sees.

He nudges Roy, and says, "Stop it, stop it, look, look here, I mean there." Roy doesn't pay any attention for a moment, then he notices no one is answering his questions and he turns around to see what we are looking at.

Less than forty yards away, standing in a line inside the low fence of their little cottage watching us recover are three of the most gorgeous sunbathing beauties we have ever seen. In high spirits [we can tell from their laughter], and friendly [they are waving and smiling], wearing only these tiny little patches of fabric concealing the obvious unknowns of man's desire for the meaning of life. One of them shouts out to us, "Bitte, geht's Sie gut? Ist irgendeiner schwer verletzt?" [which we think means, Is ya'll okay? and Is anyone badly hurt? Or, at least that's what we think she means].

Jack looks at Roy, Roy looks at Billy Wayne, Billy Wayne looks at Jack, and in the silence of that instant, we understand what we have to do, and in unison, we all start groaning, limping around, and shouting out to the Sirens of the Oberpfalz, "Hilf, bitte, hilf uns, bitte... bitte...hilf...bitte. [without a lick of shame].

That's when the Buschbohm Sisters, Adalwolfa, Adellinde, and Adelonda leap over the fence and start running toward us. In any boy's lifetime, there may be only a handful of incidents like this, when without really trying you know you have fallen backwards into one of those life long memories that you will treasure forever, and your know from that very moment on, no matter what else happens in your life, your feeble mind will spend an inordinate amount of time for the rest of your days, trying to get back to this one singular moment in time.

So, on the way back from the Dump, isolated and almost alone in the middle of a damaged Hops field, we met the Buschbohm Sisters, the Sirens of the Oberpfalz, and we lost our chance at the record for the fastest Trash Detail Run in the history of USAREUR.

5

A CASTLE HUNT

THE COOL WET air is full of mist, maybe some drizzle, some fog, too. It's like one of those old photographs from Life Magazine or the Saturday Evening Post where, if you look real close you can just make out the low slung profiles of big O.D. green battle tanks sitting idle in the mist of the German countryside, but it's not 1944, it's 1968 and it isn't war, it's just another boring weekend in the Oberpfalz.

The Oberpfalz is the hillbilly part of Bavaria, where forests and hills, some mountains and meadows conceal quiet streams, and rock ledges stained with the patina of the ages, smoke and grime on silent stone faces. Sometimes, in some places, if I just give in to my imagination, I feel it all around me, until I hear someone shout out something in German or G.I. gibberish, and I know I'm not back home there on my grandad's place up in Bee Creek Hollow.

They say hello here with their own colloquial greeting, "Gruss Gott", which means, "Greet God".

The sarcastic response from the city elite is, "Ich will wenn ich Ihn sehen", or "I will when I see Him". [just another German Master Race thing, they can't seem to get over it].

This place is different. We're are one of the few units in Europe who receive a kind of hard duty pay, an extra thirteen dollars a month, because this place is really out here in the boonies along the Czech border. Don't get us wrong, there is nothing bad about this, thirteen dollars is a lot of money here, or rather a lot of Deutsche Marks, or a lot beer.

We're all just sprawled out here in our room in the HQ Troop barracks, waiting, for what we don't know, when someone opens the door, and from the speakers on either side of the room, the Rascals hit song, 'Good Lovin' blasts out of Dave's Akai reel to reel tape deck, "ONE... TWO... THREE, GOOD LOVIN'... GOOD LOVIN'...GOOD LOVIN'...I WAS FEELIN' SO BAD..."

"What ch'all doin' today?" Pancho asks [his aka is Jacinto].

There's no response from anyone, because ever since Dave wired up the Akai to play Good Lovin' whenever the door opens, we just laugh and listen to the song.

When the tune is over, Pancho says, "Eddy says they're goin' on a castle hunt." This plays around the room like a game of pepper, he hits a glancing liner, Dave tosses it back, "Is that right?" He hits one to Pete, "Ya wanna go?" He tosses it to me, "Why not?" I toss it back to Pancho, "Let's go!" Looks like it works, everyone gets up at once.

I see Eddy & Pat [Pat is Eddy's wife] pull through the main gate in their six passenger Volkswagen Bug. Eddy is driving, Pat is in the front passenger seat, I crawl into the pocket behind the back seat, Dave, Pete & Pancho sit in the back seat.

There are more than a hundred castles in the Oberpfalz, mostly along the Naab River, but, of course, none of us know this, we just put our faith in the old adage G.I.s around here have relied on since 1945, which is, 'there must be a castle somewhere around here.' It really doesn't matter, because just getting out off the Pond for a little bit is okay. There's always another good beer out there somewhere, another strudel, another "LAS DAS, G.I.!" or something interesting.

We take off in no particular direction, then someone makes the mistake of asking, "Which way?" Eddy cuts the wheel into a tight right turn, and we turn in circles until someone else points and says, "There, that way."

We wander through the Oberpfalz, keeping our eyes peeled, scanning up along the ridge lines, the crests of hills, and occasionally checking the roadside for the next Gasthaus, the next bier, the next brat, or a strudel. It gets kinda sleepy after a while, and we stop to stretch our legs, get our bearings. That's when Pete sees it; a spire peeks out of the trees on top of the hill across the road.

"What is it, you think?" Pat asks us.

"It's a castle, it's a castle," Eddy screams.

Pancho strains to see, moves across the road, "Nah, it's just another church or somethin'."

Eddy yells out again, "No, no, it's a castle!"

Dave looks at me, "Our castle in the sky."

I look up toward the top. There's something up there, it might even be a castle. The problem is the thing is way up there at more than a sixty degree slope, straight up to the top, tangles of underbrush, bare rock in places, not something partly inebriated G.I.s ought to be climbing.

"Okay, let's go," Eddy yells. He takes off up the side of the hill pulling himself along, using the underbrush to hang onto and the rocks to push off of. It's funny; he looks like Spiderman. I look at Dave and Pancho; Pete trots after Eddy. Pat's smarter than all of us; she sits down in the car.

It isn't like there's an option anymore, we have to go. The boys are all climbing now, it isn't easy, it seems like it's getting steeper as we get half way up. We keep taking these screaming slides backwards, over rocks and brambles that tear little patches of skin away from the body. I get into a suicide slide I can't seem to stop, an uncontrolled bouncing dive, I finally catch myself on a root or something, I hold on for dear life, roll over and mumble into the sky, "Oh, my gawd, I'm cut up, I'm bleeding, I know I'm going to die."

Someone grabs my right arm, someone my left, I look up, it's Dave and Pancho, they haul me up to the next level. When we get closer, we look up to the structure, it's looks more like a castle, maybe a well built one, one that is built on a steep defensive posture with no opening on this side at all, just a shear vertical wall that goes straight up. We look back down to the road probably more than a hundred and thirty feet below, down the treacherous incline we just struggled to overcome. And, we know without even saying it, there's no way back down this thing that is survivable.

At the top there's this little space about eight inches deep, a little ledge of fate that runs the length of the vertical wall. We hang by our elbows, our fingertips, and work our way to the corner of the building, about five hundred feet from where we are. Eddy keeps saying, "it's a castle, it's a castle." No one argues with him.

At the edge of the perimeter wall, we crawl up onto a flat plain, stand up and look back over the side. We look for a little spec of blue, the VW bug, but it's gone. As we make our way around the castle, we hear some screaming and hooting and hollering from inside the place. There must be some kind of party going on inside. When we get around to the front of the place, we see a huge car park, and the entrance to the place. We trot over to the gate, a big metal latticework of a gate digs into the gravel entrance, closed shut. Eddy says, "Told ya so!"

Inside I see people milling around in a courtyard, some just stumbling along like they are in a daze. It's a pretty scruffy bunch. Some guy is dancing along in his sock feet; he's wearing a gown of some kind. Up close to the gate, this beautiful woman holds a big wad of her long hair in her mouth, and she chews on it as she hums a tune. We stare through the metal latticework

— 31 —

and wonder what the hell we're looking at, Eddy hollers at her, "Hey, hey, Ma'am. Can you let us in? Can you open up?" This startles her, she looks up, laughs, then she screams and runs off.

As we are standing there gaping at the people inside this place, someone from inside shouts, "WAS? WO? WER? JETZ! HEIR? A nun in her black habit appears, she's in a trot toward us, screaming, "RAUS, RAUS!" When she sees us up close, she stops in her tracks, turns to look for help, but there's no one to support her, and the woman we yelled at is still screaming. When the Sister turns back to us, she's very angry, "AUSSLEIGEN! DUMMSTEN! RAUS! RAUS!. She catches her breath and tries, "AUS! AUS!" Then she figures we're American, probably a bunch of G.I.s, and she gets our attention with some terms we all recognize, "LAS DAS, G.I., LAS DAS! POLIZEI! POLIZEI! [which means STOP THAT. STOP THAT! POLICE! POLICE!]

Eddy turns around with a quizzical look on his face, then the lights come on, he gets this big greasy grin on his face, and he whispers, "It's an insane asylum." He says this like it's some marvelous revelation, then, without saying anything else he takes off running across the parking lot. As we start down the incline, we all discover at the same time, that we are running down this switchback road, and we all start laughing, we can't help it, there's this big wide wonderful road all the way up to the top of this hill, and we just struggled for an hour climbing the cliff on the back side.

We only make it a few yards, before we see Pat driving up the road to get us, and she's laughing too. It's fun to be young and stupid, especially when your friends are almost as young and stupid as you are.

There were plenty of castle hunts, this one sticks out for all the obvious reasons, but there were others that were almost as much fun. We got locked in Nurnberg Castle one night, wandered around until we found an unlocked ground floor window to crawl out of. And, we found this one castle that had a caretaker who was a P.O.W. in Memphis, Tennessee for years. He treated us to the grand tour, bought us all a bier, showed us some pictures of the Mississippi River he cut out of magazines. He wants to go back there one day. He loves Elvis and Jerry Lee's music.

6

DUTY CLERK

IT'S A LITTLE room, no; it's a very narrow little room in the Headquarters building next to S-1. It stinks of ink, and rubber cement, and spirit duplicator fluid, and cigarette butts, and pencil shavings, and such. I take a deep breath, and get the dipsy dizzies. All the shelves are crammed with stuff, and in the center against one wall, there is a kind of a jump seat chair, and an ancient relic of a telephone switchboard from some 1930s movie set. You know, the kind with the headset over the ears with the mic arm and the fabric insulated pairs of wires inset on reels that you pull up, stretch out and plug in to connect someone with whomever they want to talk to. And, there's a little pale light over this board that casts ominous shadows in unexpected directions. This is where the Duty Clerk sits, all night long, yes, all night in case someone calls the 3rd Reconnaissance Squadron by landline. Hardly anyone calls the 3rd Squadron on the landline in the daytime, much less in the nighttime.

This duty is like drawing the short straw to decide who has to sit out this quarter, or this inning because the sides are uneven. The Head Shed is empty, the hours are long and silent, the relentless fumes play tricks in your mind's eye, boredom permeates the night, paralyzes your brain, and the main objective is just to stay awake.

Rarely, you hear this buzzing-ringing sensation in your ears and after a moment you realize someone is calling, you have to answer, "Specialist [state your name], 3rd Reconnaissance Squadron, 2nd Armored Cavalry, Sir. How may I direct your call, Sir?"

Usually, it's just the Adjutant calling because the C.O. makes him call to see if we're awake. Or, it could be the C.O. calling to make sure the Adjutant has called to see if we're awake. If we're awake, it's okay, if we're not we will be awake soon.

Sometimes we would like to call the C.O. to see if he is awake, but if we called and he was asleep, he would probably call us back to see if we called, or to see if we're awake.

Most of us find some unique way to stay awake. Dave [not his real name], for example, writes music, drinks coffee, walks the hall to stay alert, then if the he hears a ring, he runs to the switchboard and answers. Pete [not his real name], saves this time to write home, write Congress, write his girlfriends, write letters to the editor of the Dallas Times Herald, or he spit shines his boots. It doesn't matter what you do, as long as you stay awake.

Or, you can call some of the guys you came over here with if you know where they are. I got a hold of

Espinosa once, in Stuttgart, they went over to his room woke him up, and made him come over to the Head Shed. He asked me never to call him again. I tried to get a hold of Rega, I called Heidelberg, and asked for him, but they said he was doing six months in the Mannheim Stockade. They wouldn't tell me why, and they put some officer on the phone that wanted to know my name. I hung up.

In the daytime the land lines here are terrible, if you can't hear the person on the other end of the line, you holler at him, and if they shout back their voices get distorted and there's a lot of static, so we all digress to the fail safe, we have to yell out what we want using the phonetic alphabet. You know, Tango Hotel India Sierra…India Sierra…Sierra Papa Echo Charlie India Alpha Lima India Sierra Tango… Charlie Oscar Lima Echo Mike Alpha November [or, This is Specialist Coleman, by shouting each letter]. This sometimes makes for a very long conversation, but if you have nothing else to do, it's not so bad, you can get your message across even if you don't have the patience to wait for a response.

The only calls you can really hear well are the calls we receive at night, or local calls from the Germans. This is even more infrequent than a nighttime call from someone at regiment, usually just the local Polizei telling us to come pick up our guys that they have arrested. This duty is almost always a duty for the Personnel Office staff.

This time it was Eddy's turn. It was especially quiet that night [it was snowing and this happened before

Patricia got to Germany]. It was getting cold outside, at
1930 hours the boredom was already ankle deep, and
there were still ten and a half hours to go. The only thing
that was working for Eddy was his yo-yo, then the string
broke. As he rummaged through this Supply/S-1 Mail
Mimeograph/Switchboard Room shelves, he heard
that distinctive ringing noise. He had to look around
for his headset, it was on the floor. When he answered,
"Specialist Parker, 3rd Reconnaissance Squadron, Sir,"
a German voice interrupted him,

The voice said, "Hallo."

Surprised by the clarity of the call, Eddy just listened, and after a few moments he managed to say,
"Hallo."

"Hallo," the voice again.

"HALLO," Eddy again.

"Guten Abend, mein namen ist Frederick."

"HALLO, this is Eddy."

"Mein Frau und mich mochten wissen…"

"WAS [the German for, What]," Eddy still shouting.

"Entshuldigen, Sie. [then a sound like someone
unrolling a piece of paper, and the voice goes into the
sound of someone reading] "My namen is Fred… und
my Frau und Ich… vould like to… invite an Amerikanish
G.I. to… our home… for Christmas dinner. Can you…
hilf me?"

Almost immediately Eddy understands what he has
to do. "Wunderbar! My namen is Eddy, what day is this
dinner?" Over the next few minutes Eddy sold out his
komrades, accepted the invitation for himself, and got
the details of where and when Fred would pick him up.

He tried to keep this under his hat, but he couldn't help himself, he started bragging about it. And, after everyone else knew what had happened, they started in on Eddy.

"Nice going, Eddy. Did you ever think that your ol' Komrade there just wants some G.I. to exchange for his brother-in-law over there behind the Iron Curtain?"

Or, "Yeah, thanks Eddy, be sure to carry the phone number for U.S. Embassy in Prague with you, so you can maybe get them to negotiate for your release."

Eddy tried to laugh off these remarkably cynical ideas, but they just wouldn't go away. Then, the nightmares came, the mysterious man in dark clothes, wearing sunglasses, nervous acting, would stop his car where Eddy stood and jump out and stick a gun in his ribs, and he would wake up. Then he would laugh at himself, go back to scoffing at the idea again, then he would wake up in a sweat. Finally, he figured it was worth the chance, and he stood out front of the Main Gate one day with a little package of coffee and cigarettes under his arm.

When Fred pulls up and gets out of his car, he is very friendly, maybe too friendly, and he is wearing those sunglasses and he keeps looking at his watch. With a stupid grin on his face Eddy manages to get himself into the car, and as they roar off toward the Czech border, Eddy thinks maybe this is it for me.

A little ways down the road at a phone booth, Fred pulls over and says he has to make a call. Eddy can only think that maybe he is setting up the exchange. It's now that he remembers he has a Top Secret clearance, but of course, he doesn't know anything, he has nothing to exchange for his freedom, but they probably will think he does, he knows they'll torture him, and his mind races ahead of himself, but he can't get out of its way.

He thinks about home, he thinks about Pat, he thinks about getting out and running, but he can't move, his legs won't help him. He just sits there, terrified. Fred gets back in the car, and a few miles, and a few minutes later he pulls up in front of a house in Ursensollen, the next village over, and Eddy makes life long friends with Fred und Oochie. Fred's brother-in-law had escaped on his own, without any help from anyone.

7

Count de Money

Lieutenant 3G, the lieutenant with three first names, shouldn't be on active duty in anyone's army, but unfortunately, he is. He's in our army. I see him scooting across the parade field, always in a hurry, he kind of scrambles around from place to place wherever he goes, but you have to look real close to see if he actually picks up his feet. He doesn't look to the right, to the left, he doesn't ever look over his shoulder, and sometimes he doesn't even look up. He stares at the ground directly in front of him, and more often than not when he finally gets someplace, it probably isn't the place he was going when he started out.

But, he somehow makes his way around in fits and starts until he finds himself in the place he wants to be. If you see him out there anywhere, and try to salute him, you may or may not get a salute in return, or you may get one of his shocked and startled salutes, or you could get one of his longer than necessary salutes, or you may get more than one salute, you just have to be prepared for whatever comes your way, because Lieutenant 3G is never sure what he's doing or where he is.

For the most part, whatever he does is sort of inconsequential, because everyone knows he shouldn't be put in a position where he would have to think about what he's doing, or how to do it. Early on, they took away his cavalry saber, because the bill of his cap, and his nose was always banged up and bleeding from his attempts at 'Present Arms'. So, mostly he's the designated utility infielder for the entire Squadron. He stays in, in his room in the BOQ, in his office next to the Service Club, in the Officer's Club if there is no one else there, but always on the Pond, always on the Pond, never out anywhere off the Pond. Well, never out since that one fateful day he was assigned the duty of 3rd Reconnaissance Squadron Payroll Officer.

Each month the designated Squadron Payroll Officer takes two guys from the Personality Shop, finds a jeep, and a footlocker, and they drive up to 14th Finance at Regiment in Nurnberg. When they get there, they count out about two-hundred and fifty thousand in Deutsche Marks and United States Dollars American. They sign for this payroll, put it in the footlocker, and drive back to the Pond.

This massive waste of time, and this unnecessary risk is kind of a United States Army thing. You have to understand that traditions in the Army die slow, long, hard deaths, and some of them you just can't kill. One of them is this Pay Day ritual; they even have a bugle call for this, Pay Call. All of us in the Personality

Shop get paid by check directly from Fort Benjamin Harrison back stateside each month, and we usually get our checks days before Payroll is issued in the cash form, but all the others wait for it from 14th Finance.

This is okay duty in the summer, a little on the brisk side in the spring and fall and sometimes scary and cold in the winter [diving in a jeep on frozen roads]. The only fun thing about it is speculating on the idea of stealing the *p*ayroll, and getting away with it. As of yet, we have not come up with a fool proof plan for enriching our circumstances by the diversion of the *p*ayroll to our own use, however, we are still working on the details.

Pete and Olin get the Pay Day duty on this particular day, Lieutenant 3G. gets it by default. Somehow, by the mysteries of chance, he's the only officer available for this duty. Pete found a footlocker, Olin went over to the motor stables and got the jeep, they met LT 3G at the Headquarters Troop armory where they drew their weapons. This duty requires that each trooper in the detail be armed with a .45 caliber pistol with a full magazine. However, there is no requirement that the trooper or officer who is issued a .45 caliber side arm is qualified with this weapon, or even knows how to use it. Upon LT 3G's request, and against the objections of Olin, Pete is ordered to show LT 3G how to load his weapon.

14th Finance is located at regiment in Merrell Barracks in Nurnberg. It's about 60 Klicks from Amberg. Merrell Barracks is named for Pvt. Joseph F. Merrell posthumously awarded the Congressional

Medal of Honor [CMH] for heroic action in battles near Lohe, Germany, April, 1945.

This place is another old Nazi Kaserne; an SS Kaserne named the Sued Kaserne. It is pretty much shot up from its capture in 1945, all the holes are still there. In the front façade and at the main gate you can still see where missing chunks of cast stone knocked out by deflected bullets have left these little craters in this structure's facade. Driving into his place everyone gets a feeling in their guts like this is a very special place, a place where we lost American lives in the struggle to capture it.

The trip to Merrell Barracks is uneventful. Upon arrival at 14th Finance each group is instructed to clear their weapons, meaning unload the weapons before we move about the building. While Pete and Olin are doing this, LT 3G takes it upon himself to figure out how to unload his weapon.

Unmedicated and unsupervised, LT 3G's grip on his receiver slips and he discharges his weapon in the lobby of 14th Finance. The bullet ricochets around the room, missing all fifteen people in the foyer, until it gets lodged in the wall over where Pete's head had been moments earlier, but now Pete's head is plastered to the floor next to Olin's head and about eight other guys nearby. There is dead silence in the lobby; everyone kind of takes inventory to see if they still have all their pieces. and that there aren't any holes leaking vital fluids. Then, they look around to see if everyone else can move. They all look okay, and there is no blood pooling up under anyone, then someone in authority shouts, "IS ANY ONE HIT? IS ANY ONE HIT?" There was no response, and a collective sigh of relief spills out of the mouths of the survivors.

The silence is shattered again by a much deeper, much more agitated voice of a higher authority, "All right, all right, who did it? Who did it? Where is he? Where is he? Where is the poor dumb son-of-a-bitch. NOW! NOW!"

LT 3G surrenders quietly, raises his hand, and climbs up the stairs, and follows the Commanding Officer of 14th Finance into the dark recesses of the building. There is a low constant rumble from the depths of 14th Finance that lasts for a long, long time, there is pounding, and loud noises punctuated with bangs, and bumps of material hitting walls and floors. Then, silence again, a loud banging noise, another long silence, then, nothing.

In the Army, there is a price to pay when something like this happens, and the price is paid in many ways, one of which is paper, miles and miles of paper, scrawled out in long hand with confessions and signatures, and details out the wazzoo by the perpetrators, the witnesses, the innocent bystanders, the staff, the visitors, and any one in a radius of sight, earshot, blast range, or any one else in close proximity to the event. You also have to pay in time, because no one who discharges a weapon indoors at 14th Finance is going to be allowed to do any counting of money until the very last detail of the very last unit has finished their count and left to return to their post.

So, Pete and Olin and LT 3G sit for hours writing, and waiting and explaining, and hoping and praying until someone finally lets them get back to work and count out the payroll for the 3rd Herd.

In the aftermath of this all day ordeal, and after missing lunch, and waiting for so long, they finally get the money counted out, and pack it away in the footlocker,.Pete gets the LT's weapon and returns it to him, unloaded, and Pete loads his weapon, Olin loads his, and they get back on the road to the Pond after dark.

Somewhere near Ursensollen, exhausted and hungry, they pull over at a little gasthaus for some grub. Under the burdens of the day, they all get out and go inside, the place is full of Germans celebrating someone's good fortune. They order and wait. Then, Pete looks up at Olin, Olin looks back at Pete, they both look at LT 3G, and they all realize at the same moment, they left the pay roll sitting there all alone in the jeep. Then, without saying anything, in a fit of sheer terror, they all jump up and run out to the jeep to see if their footlocker is still chained to the jeep and the padlock is still in place on the lid.

Still there. Without a word, they wipe the sweat off, and get back in the jeep and don't stop until they get home to the Pond.

LT 3G is never the same after this, not that anyone could really tell for sure if anything changed, but we see less and less of him until one day he just evaporates in the ether. Olin says to put him on TDY [Temporary Duty] to Ulm, no one can pronounce Ulm anyway, so no one is likely to ask any questions, and we leave it like that until we can all rotate out of here, and let the next group decide what to do about it.

We do this, but every time I see a little guy shuffling along, head down, and hardly picking up his feet, I try to figure out how I can get as far away from him as fast as possible and stay there, because as I understand it, he never turned in his weapon.

8

WE MEASURE TIME

WE MEASURE OUR time here in all kinds of ways. If we have a favorite pastime, it is finding another new way to count down to the day we rotate back to the States, the day we go home. I don't know why this is, but I think it might be one way of distracting our attention away from being here, and it nurtures the corrupted ideals of our girlfriends, and families, and all the friends we left behind. Of course, this time obsession doesn't work like we want it to. We all keep these little memories going on in the back of our mind, or at least, we hold something back, reserve a piece of our past, so maybe we won't do something stupid like reenlist, or something reckless like having so much "fun" we get caught or arrested and/or detained in civilian or military custody.

In keeping with our time obsession, most everyone here smokes. Cigarettes are only two bucks a carton, and American cigarettes are excellent bartering items.. We can get most anything we want with a few packs of

Marlboros. Since almost everyone smokes, we all carry cigarette lighters, mostly a Zippo, or a Ronson. Zippos, well, because they are Zippos, and Ronsons, because of the sorta of oval shape that just a little momentum causes it to keep rolling. This is important for the Ronson Races. Ronson Races are a high stakes contest of endurance and speed. I'll get back here in a moment, so don't lose this.

The German beer bottles here are unique, and unless your grandmother canned the vegetables from her garden, you've probably never seen anything like the way the German beer bottle is capped. Each bottle is topped off with a wire bail holding a ceramic plug tight against the top with a red washer sealing in the beer. To open a German beer bottle, you simply grab the neck and push on the wire bail with your thumb to release it and the top flips off and hangs over the bottle neck by the wire bail.

The rubber washers on the beer bottles become another unit of measure for the time we are here. For every six months in USAREUR, we take one of the washers and stretch it around our Zippo or our Ronson. Then, if someone asks for a light, we just pull out our lighters and light their cigarette. By doing this everyone can see if we are just a raw recruit or a veteran. And, the bonus is that no matter what inexplicable position we might wind up in with our pants on or off, the rubber washers keep our lighter from slipping out of our pocket.

Of course, this trick eliminates some of the fun of answering the question, "How long have you been overseas?" With our washers in place, you don't get to say stuff like, "How long? Hey, man I was a DRO [Dining Room Orderly] at the Last Supper." Or, "Hey, man when I got here this was an Army of Occupation."

Another less visible unit of measure for our time over here is the accumulation of German beer mugs. A German beer mug is a solid glass container capable of holding one liter of beer, that's about a quart in real world terms. And, we're not talking here about the tourist bier stein with the lid, we're talking about the real thing, the clear glass chunk of mug with no lid, no ornamentation, and certainly no music box.

This mug can be used for many things, one of which is drinking beer. It can also double as a collector's item enhancing the décor of any barracks room, American attic, basement, dorm, or bookshelf. In emergencies, it can also be deployed as a weapon, a paperweight, a goldfish bowl, or wheel chocks for a vehicle on a steep incline, a nutcracker, an ashtray, a coin bank, or even as a bail if your boat is sinking.

Some guys measure their time here by the number of beer mugs they have collected. This might become a less than practical approach for some of the R.A.s [the Regular Army troops] the enlistees, and even the A.U.S.s [the Army of the United States troops], better known as the draftees as boh have to carefully consider the bulk and space that may be involved in accumulating too many of these. Nevertheless, there is something compelling about the idea of having this hunk of glass. These mugs are a solid reminder of many of the great things about our time here, and we have to admit, we really cherish the idea of keeping some of them as souvenirs of our time over here in Deutschland.

So, no beer fest [a Beer Festival] goes unnoticed by the G.I.s on the Pond. At this type of function the big attraction for us is the cost of the beer, it is next to nothing, and as always the opportunity to get another mug or two. These are very appealing features to any G.I. Most of these events are local festivals that occur mostly without warning, and since we aren't always on the list of invitees to an upcoming fest, we are always on the lookout, because as far as we know, a fest might break out any time.

On one of the highest peaks surrounding Amberg there is a Franciscan monastery and church, Mariahilfberg [Our Lady of Help]. The steep climb to the top is made possible for most everyone by a paved path rising modestly in each 8 to 10 foot section with long wide inclined pavers in between each low rise step that make the climb to the top as accessible as possible. Along this path are the fourteen Stations of the Cross, the Via Dolorosa of this church and monastery. Once a year, the monastery hosts a Bier Fest, a celebration of the products of the monastery. This is the same church where Pat & Eddy, and Gail & Roy were married. I think that's how we found out about this fest.

When we arrive, it is still daylight and everything is just getting underway. Behind the monastery long rows of picnic tables are set up under single bulb string lights like the ones at the county fair. Kegs of bier are within easy reach of almost every table, just a few steps away. There is, naturally, an OOM-Pah band playing all the iconic favorites.

We drink, we sing along with the Germans on the songs we know. We drink, and after a while we sing along with them on the ones we don't know. We drink, and lock arms and sway back and forth when everyone else does. All this drinking and singing, and swaying gets all the old Germans really wound up.

The old German national anthem, the *Deutschland, Deutschland Uber Alles is* still forbidden in Germany, but looking around this place, we can see that doesn't set well with these folks, I also think it's tough for them to sit here with us, an ever present reminder of the war and all the nasty associations that period holds. There are still plenty of Nazis here in Germany in the late sixties, and they seem to manifest their loyalties when encouraged by alcohol and music. We don't pay much attention to this, but sometimes we can't avoid it. There is this deep dark streak of passionate nationalism in the German character that must be hard for them to suppress. And, as always there are way too many plain old fanatics here.

I'm sitting at this long row of picnic tables filled with G.I.s, my guess is about sixty to seventy of us are here. Everyone is having a great time and no one wants this to end anytime soon. On this long row of tables, there must be more than twice the number of mugs as G.I.s., and the effects of this much alcohol is starting to show itself. The Franciscian brothers must see the same things I see, and without warning, the lights go out. This is the signal that this fest is over, and everyone should get up and head home. The lights only stay off for a few seconds, but this is long enough for all of the mugs and almost all of the G.I.s to disappear. When the lights come back on, I'm sitting here by myself at an empthy table, and I do mean empty, there are no mugs in sight, there are no G.I.s on this particular row of tables, even the mug that I was drinking from has disappeared.

It takes a few seconds for this to sink in with the rest of the crowd, and just as the shouting and yelling start, I get the heck out of there. Only one drunken Nazi follows me, but despite his inebriated state he manages to keep up with me somehow. I don't yet understand drunken German, the language, which is just as well, because I don't think he does either. I do make out that he is a Wehrmacht veteran, a Feldwebel [Staff Sergeant], with campaign experience on both the Ostfront and the Westfront, but that's about it. He stumbles as much as I do, him because he's drunk, me because I can't see well after dark. Finally, he quits trying to get up, and I leave him at the top of the Via Dolorosa.

I do the Via Dolorosa backwards, I pick my way down the hill in measured steps trying to keep on the paved path that I know is there somewhere under me, and I know it will take me to the bottom near the Kaiser Wilhelm Ring. I also have the benefit of honing in on the raucous crowd far ahead of me as they sing their way home repeating all the favorites, *Ein Prosit*, *Lilli Marleen*, and *Lola*. As we wander through the streets of Amberg, lights in homes go on and then off, an occasional curse echoes through a once peaceful street from a window, or doorway, and then in the distance I hear the sirens of the Polizei wailing along in the night.

By the time I catch up with everyone at the Main Gate of the Pond, there is this long wavy and unstable line. Two Polizei cars are parked there with their trunks open, and everyone is surrendering their mugs in order to get back in the gate. Inside the Pond, the O.D. [Officer of the Day] is there kicking ass and taking names. He seems like he's embarrassed, but he might be just irritated that he had to get out of bed and come down here. As folks surrender the mugs, and check in with the O.D., I see there must be more than a hundred mugs in the trunks of the Polizei's cars. The O.D. sends us all into the Headquarters building, and after an impromptu lecture on German-American relations, the negative effects fo an International Incidents, and numerous threats, we get sent to our respective rooms. When we leave the Head Shed, Dave is right there beside me, we're talking about the bier fest, or at least I am because somewhere along the way I lose Dave but don't know it, and I only understand this as it becomes more and more of a one sided conversation. When I get to the barracks, I look up and he's just gone.

Inside, as I'm telling the guys about our unsuccessful bier mug heist, the drunken Nazi, doing the Via Dolorosa backwards and the confiscation of all of the mugs, Dave walks into our room with two of the mugs he managed to smuggle in the front gate under his jacket, and when the O.D. sent us to the Head Shed, he ducked into the Latrine and tossed them out the back window, retrieving them when we were on the way to the barracks.

This is what the Nazis hated about fighting Americans, they never knew what they were going to do next, many times these G.I.s ignored orders [something a German simply cannot do], and right in the middle of a battle, G.I.s did unexpected things like stop and smoke a cigarette, and unlike the Germans, if an officer or noncom went down, the next guy in line [even if he was only a Private] took over command of the unit, and they kept fighting. No matter the objective, they found a way to do what they set out to do.

So, in keeping with the spirit and tenacity of our forefathers, Specialist Dave, without regard for his own personal safety or possible nonjudicial punishment, under heavy scrutiny by the Franciscan monks, the drunken Nazis, the Polizei, the O.D., under cover of darkness, and undaunted by the overwhelming forces assembled against him, he used his inherent innovative spirit, and maneuvered himself under heavy opposition to prevail against these overwhelming odds, liberating two more bier mugs from German captivity. Therefore, in the best traditions of the United States Army, the 2nd Armored Cavlary, and Reminton's Raiders, Specialist 5 Dave is awarded this token of recognition for his exceptional thirst and relentless obsession.

Anyone with as many bier mugs as Dave has, well, he just been here way too long.

9

FIRE IN THE HOLE

WE DIDN'T KNOW it then, but the six precious hours of sleep we got that night was all we would get for days. Not that we noticed, not until just before we collapsed back on our bunks almost fully dressed, and still confused.

A plume of black smoke swirled up out of the Motor Stables behind the S-4 building that morning. I put my coffee cup down and went over to the window. It didn't look like much, but I was more than two hundred yards out, and it was a beautiful day in the Oberpfalz. I turned around to announce my discovery, and with the word, "Hey…" the sound of the first blast and the concussion wave slammed through the building and my body.

I lost my mind for a moment, and I kept standing there with my imaginary thumb up my imaginary butt trying to figure out these strange sensations as my internal organs settled back into place. When I found my mind it was already in the basement of the Headquarters building, and T.J. was the only one that beat it down there. In the time it took for us to move forty-five feet from the office to the basement, another round went off which for some inexplicable reason made us giggle, but it wasn't one of those funny giggles, it was one of those terrified giggles like the kind you get just before the trap door opens up and you tumble into the abyss.

Jim, a new arrival to our office who is Vietnam vet, and Pete were outside walking along toward the Headquarters Troop barracks. Along this walkway, there is a "keep off the grass" barrier, little red stakes that stick out of the ground a couple of feet with a single string run through the top portion about eighteen inches off the grass. Pete says, when the first blast wave hit them, he watched dumbfounded as Jim dived under the little string without even touching the ground or the string. His guess is, this is how you know if you really talking to a veteran or just another guy on the street.

Then, there was a weird silence. Nothing, no one moved, even the air was still for a few seconds. Then came the third blast, a double-double, maybe, it felt like the building stood up, then flopped back down with us in it. The concussion found its way into the basement, and rattled around down here with us for a moment. Only then did we hear the wail of the sirens.

The Commo Sergeant bounded down into the basement, opened up the commo storage area, and disappeared inside its dark recesses. Then, he sprang out with a Prick 25 in each hand. We, T.J. and I, edged our way along the hallway to the stairway. We got ourselves about half way up the steps when another round exploded, and we dived back into our cushy lair.

The Commo Sergeant kept making regular dashes in and out of the basement until he spotted us huddled together there on the floor. He stopped in his tracks, studied us for a second, looked up toward the outside, looked back down at us again, and said without any voice inflection at all, "You two guys are the smartest guys in this whole damn Squadron," and he sprinted back into the action.

"What the hell is going on out there?" T.J. says this like I know something, but I don't.

All I can think is, "That fire up there, that was in the area where How Battery parks their stuff."

"You think one of those 109s blew up? You think one of those 109s blew up?" T.J. says, T.J. says.

An M109 is a self propelled Howitzer with a 155mm cannon. The thing weights about 27 tons, and carries a basic load of 28-32 artillery rounds, including HE [High Explosive], WP [White Phosphorus, or Willie Peter], Anti-Personnel HE rounds, Illumination Rounds, and Signal/Smoke Rounds. The thing looks like a tank with an oversized turret and cannon mounted on top the tracks.

Out of nowhere, we heard a German siren [you know the uuuh-ahhh, uuuh-ahhh, uuuh-ahhhh sound] heading our way, and we crawled up the stairs again to take a peek. Three West German Fire Trucks came roaring in the main gate, lights flashing, sirens wailing. They got almost up to the S-4 building before another round went off, and they made this remarkable about face and roared right back past us and out the main gate, lights flashing, sirens blaring.

Pete and Jim low crawled their way into the basement with T.J. and me and we all started talking at once, but no one could actually hear or understand what anyone else was saying and this went on until we ran out of breath. It took a while for us to figure out that we sounded like this because no one could hear anything or anyone in the atermath of these explosions, or over the high pitched ringing in our ears.

Every so often, another round would suspend us in anticipation long enough for the ringing in our ears to subside a little, then the whole wait, listen, watch, giggle, talk fast over each other thing would start over again. Every now and then, the Germans would show up in their fire trucks, crawl up the road toward the S-4 building ever so slowly until another round went off, then they would roar back out of the Pond again like they were on fire.

I wondered where everyone else was, I wondered how many of us were just blown away, I wondered how many were hurt, but all I could really think about was this phrase that kept scrolling through my head, it read, "Okay, we're alive, Okay, we're still alive, Okay, we're Okay, I think," in between giggles.

The basement of the HQ building is where the PAL-CRYPTO message center is; this is a good place to go when things like this happen. The structure is reinforced to protect the message center from a direct hit. I don't know how long we were down there, but it was a long time. Sergeant Tyler brought some messages down to the message center and found us.

"Okay, Kiddies, it's Showtime, let's get going."

We went outside and stood around gazing up toward the Motor Stables. Smoke was still rising from the site, but now it was white smoke instead of black. The Sarge said it's all over with up there, but it's just beginning for us, and we adjourned to the office for our assignments and a briefing. Pete and Dave were sent up to the site to secure the area for investigators, they told us later all that was left of a 27 ton Howitzer was the base plate and a few road wheels holding on the last bits of track left underneath them. Sergeant Tyler took a team downtown to gather injury/damage data from the locals, we set up seven interview stations in the personnel office, Joe and Jim organized, prioritized, and set up waiting lines outside the office, T.J. and Roy started copying maps of the Motor Stables, and the rest of us started copying incident reports and rounding up pens, pencils, markers, and such for everyone to use. Someone intelligent went over to the Mess Hall and got a few trays of food, and we started interviewing people that same afternoon.

Army Incident Reports are really simple objective forms, "What did you do wrong? Why did you do that? Where exactly were you when it happened? What should you have done instead? Draw a diagram of the site, identify your position, identify the position of the other personnel there, identify the position of the equipment on this map, describe the damage, describe what your responsibility is in relation to this damage, is there anything that you could have done differently?"

And, even if you are only an innocent bystander, say you just saw some piece of the incident, heard some piece of the incident, are wearing some piece of the incident, were close enough to feel some piece of the incident, or know someone who did, you have to complete this form to the best of your ability. Then a personnel specialist, one of us, reviews it with each witness and embellishes it as necessary adding the special effects and interesting color to an otherwise flatly stated narrative. As the hours rolled on and on this commentary got more colorful and more fantastic.

You know with little phrases like, "Ka-Boom Ka-Boom", and "uhhh-ahhh, uhhh-ahhh" sirens, and little side notes like, "without regard for my own personal safety," and "my ears are still ringing," and "large pieces of jagged metal and clods of dirt were falling from the sky," and "...all I could think about was Alice." After this, an officer reviews the statements, then the individual signs and dates it, and swears that all the details are true and correct to the best of his knowledge and/or understanding.

All this time is spent on these 788 military points of view and as many civilians who want to make a claim for injury and/or damage [in this case 177 immediate claims, more later] and the work is done. Oh, yeah, and this begins immediately following the incident, and it ends when it ends.

As it turns out, the crew working on the electrical system in this track decided to take a short cut, and not bother to unload and remove the basic load of ordnance/ ammunition before they began their work on the electrical system. After all, 32 rounds at 98 pounds each is a pretty hefty load, and this group had three tracks to work on that day.

And, besides, "We never started a fire on a howitzer before, so why worry about it now?" Well, they did start a fire, and when the fire got beyond them, they ran off like any sane person would. In the end, we were missing, 13 men on sick call with various wounds described as moderate to superficial; one M109 Self-Propelled Howitzer; 5 trucks [2 Five ton trucks and three deuce and a half trucks], and one jeep.

Of course, the confessions of the repair crew sealed their fate, and we took all the paperwork down to Courts and Boards as soon as we were finished. In the final analysis, thankfully, no one was seriously injured, no one was killed, and even though one of the hatches on the track wound up crashing through the window of an elementary school downtown, the kids were not hurt, just very excited about their new experience, and they got to see the crazy Americans come around and take their picture, and board up their window, and pick up their flying Howitzer hatch and take it away.

I don't think anyone had time to look up in the two days and hours it took us to record these details. Towards the end of it, most of us were so ragged out we let any witness who wanted to ramble on and on about any and everything that was on their mind [after this many hours their imaginations took over and they just couldn't stop] even if it had nothing to do with the explosion. One guy read me the letters he had written his girlfriends back home while he was standing in line.

Pretty racy stuff and he, of course, had to show me the pictures of his intended recipients. They were all gorgeous, he was funny, and I often wonder what became of them.

During all this commotion, the Commanding Officer and the Executive Officer were off post in a meeting in Nurnburg at Regimental Headquarters, so we were lucky. The man In charge was our Adjutant, 1st Lieutenant Mike, who is the most level headed and competent officer in our unit. Without him, this could have been a real crisis, but with him there it seemed like this was just an ordinary thing that we had to do, and everyone just did there job. He never broke a sweat.

When the C.O. and the X.O. returned that day, they never came out of his offices. They spent most of their time on the phone, standing there at attention, with their heels locked, getting their ass eaten out by regiment, VII Corps, USAREUR, NATO, and sundry other generals up and down the chain of command who had nothing better to do that particular day.

I caught a glimpse of the C.O. through his partially opened office door on one of my trips down to Courts and Boards. His face was a deep dark shade of red you rarely see in nature, and as we all were, he was wilting under the pressure of an extraordinarily long and remarkable few days.

It didn't occur to me until we were walking back over to our barracks after the last bit of paperwork was completed. And, all of a sudden it popped into my head, I had missed my one singular opportunity of a lifetime to yell out that standard of the military, that one simple phrase that I always wanted to yell out, and really mean it, and I understood that I missed my chance to do it, to yell out, "FIRE IN THE HOLE!"

So, betrayed by my own feeble mind, I just did it, I yelled it out, and that's when they turned on me.

10

THE GASTHAUS
OCCUPATION MEDAL

ONLY A SELECT group of people have ever been awarded
the GOM [the Gasthaus Occupation Medal], mostly
because only this select group of people knows of such
a thing as the Gasthaus Occupation Medal. Only this
group knows about this medal because this group con-
ceived, and designed it and only the members of this
select group have ever awarded it to anyone.

The group I'm referencing here is, The Personality
Shop troops of the 3rd Herd, or more succinctly, us.
This medal is only given in recognition of the great sac-
rifices made, not exactly to earn this medal, but more
to survive the ordeal this medal is awarded for.

The actual medal is a huge hunk of burnished brass
depicting the front grill of a '58 Ford Thunderbird
with little diamond chips inset where the headlights
would be, and the grill is surrounded by a laurel wreath
made of stars, hanging from a burnished brass bar by

a multi-colored ribbon with a broad red stripe down the center, bracketed by narrower navy blue stripes alongside the red, Next to the blue stripes a pair of peachy orange stripes run alongside the blue, and on both edges are broader deep but bright pink stripes. The red represents the blood spilled, the navy blue represents the depressing aftermath of this ordeal, the peachy orange represents the volumes of beer and schnapps consumed, and the deep but bright pink represents the embarrassment and humiliation it takes to be awarded this medal.

This is not to say that each recipient of this award is not proud of his accomplishment, but if he is ever asked, just exactly if and when he was awarded this honor, he will most likely deny that he knows what you are talking about or quite flatly refute any knowledge of what you mean. If pressed further, beware of the possible consequences and further be wary of the referral that might be made by accusing so and so, or what's his name is the one you should be talking to.

The GOM, if it actually exists, is bestowed on these select few in recognition of their selfless service on behalf of their comrades in arms. And, let me say right now that there is no greater burden, no exemplary dedication to duty, no unacknowledged bitter experience more noble or gallant than this singular solitary act of devotion and sacrifice.

Civilians often ask their veteran friends what exactly they did while serving in the United States Armed Forces, and many will tell them of their exploits, their accomplishments, their awards and share with pride the meaning and purpose of each ribbon clamped together on their chest, e.g. the NDSM, the GCMDL, the ACM, the RVNCM, the VSM, CWSM, the Marksmanship badge, the Presidential Unit Citations and so on and so forth, but no one will ever tell you they have won *the* GOM. You can be sure, if they do, they have no idea what they are talking about. So, please understand, along with the pride we may share in our accomplishments, this particular award is, was, and will always be the best kept secret in the whole of the United States Armed Forces for reasons which will shortly become obvious to you.

We believe there are at least 3 to 5 personalities claiming the name Sergeant First Class George Tyler. One is a Personnel Sergeant in the 3rd Herd, the others just stepped out of one of those films from the thirties or forties one day, and became real. The genre of film noir comes to mind first, one of the classics, or some say he's more like a William Powell, or maybe a Bogart all cleaned up. Anyway, this multifaceted personality lives a complicated and adventurous existence punctuated with schemes, characters, plots, secrets, and a supporting cast as intricate and devious as any Hitchcock movie we've ever seen.

Each of us learns this by accident, and no one ever really talks about it afterwards. It just happens one day, and that innocent naïve expression that most of us come here with dissolves into the prematurely grave face of the corrupted and banal.

You know how the old folks down the street go on about stuff like this, "Well, all I know is he left here a kid, and he came back home a man." It's something like this kind of thing only different.

We see it happen almost three times a month, we get to the office, make the bratwurst run, complete the Morning Report, drink some coffee, fill out some forms, then, one of the George Tyler's springs in the door, runs through his routine, checks this out, gets on the phone, looks at that, gets caught up and sits down for a few minutes. The place gets real quiet, waiting to see which George it is, and as time ticks away, people find a sudden need to go over to S-4 for something, or they have to get down to Courts and Boards, or they suddenly have to go on Sick Call, or they try to disappear into the woodwork, but it doesn't work, none of it.

A George, one of the crazy ones, just looks up all of a sudden, scans the room, picks out an idle mind, focuses in on him and shouts, "Okay, Hot Shot, let's go." What this means is that ever whom he chooses is with him for the rest of the day, and it will be a long day. Everyone else breathes a sigh of relief and shoots side-long glances of appreciation at the victim, acknowledging his sacrifice, trying to show their admiration and at the same time thanking their lucky stars it's you and not one of them.

At first, we think, well maybe today might be different, maybe things won't get out of hand this time, maybe I can steer him clear of this place or that place, or that gal with the SS tattoo, or the place out there by the lake, but this is only a pipe dream. George goes where George wants to go, sees whomever he wants to see, and no amount of tactical or strategic distraction is going to change that.

It isn't all bad, George has a '58 Thunderbird convertible, and in this day and age, it don't get much better than this. With the top down, the wind in your face, no speed limit on the autobahn, an adventure on your mind, you decide, it might be fun this time, and it is, it's just too much fun for most of us.

George has a gregarious and fun loving nature. People, all kinds of people, gravitate towards this marvelous, whirling sphere of influence, and once they get here, they get sucked up in the vortex of his celebrity, and personality. And, once here, they just never want to go away. They said Hitler was a charismatic character, but I don't think he was ever lauded for this fun loving spirit. Well, that's the difference here, George has that charisma thing in spades, and not only that, you have to like him, you just can't help yourself, because you know, no matter what happens, it probably isn't going to be fatal, even if he looks like he might be especially dangerous today.

This feeling of euphoria might last through the first three or four stops, then things always start spinning out of control. I think the expression is, 'A beer and a bump', but even if you spent all day every day with George you never hear this phrase spoken. You never have to hear this, because when they see George coming, they just start setting things up and no sooner does your butt hit the bench in the booth, than some gorgeous blond Aryan bombshell sets a beer and a shot down in front of you, and you never see it coming, it's like magic.

Through this veil of schnapps and bier, I'm never quite sure where we are until I get close enough to catch the scent of a fräulein, or I feel a gentle kiss on my cheek. So, for some reason every time I go along with George, before I know it, I've fallen madly in love with a Gisele, or an Aixa, or an Elke, or a Bruna, or a Liesel, or any of the others except for one, Erika. Erika was just too much; she bit me on my shoulder and nearly broke my knee, she got me in a headlock and wouldn't let go. I mean this girl was determined, and if I could have understood German better than I did then, I would tell you why, but I'm not sure that matters anyway.

One thing about all this, well actually two things, about all this frolicking about in the German country-side always fascinated me. One thing was that people were always putting envelopes in George's pockets, and every single girl I met whenever I was with George always began the conversation something like this, "Wie gehts, meine Liebling. Kommen Sie doch herein!" Then, as soon as I was all in, they would cuddle up close to me, and whisper in my ear, "Kennen Sie meine Cowboy, Peer? Wo ist Peer heute?" Which I think means, 'Do I know that Cowboy, Pete? and, "Where is Pete today?" I guess Erika didn't like my answers about the Cowboy. As I tried to explain to her that the real Cowboys come from Cowtown in Fort Worth, not Dallas, but this only seemed to make her more ferocious.

All of these little excursions ended the same way. George has an internal clock and alarm system. I believe he had this system installed because he is married to a German girl with big arms who, if she wanted to, could get a man down and kill 'em. It didn't matter to George what condition his accomplice was in. Usually we couldn't actually stand up straight, speak well enough to be understood, or find the floor with both of our feet, but this didn't matter. George always knew when it was time to go, and we always made it back to the Pond just before Retreat. This big beautiful Ford Thunderbird would scream through the main gate, come to a screeching halt in front of Headquarters Troop, the door would fly open, and we would be rolled out onto the sidewalk. Then George would make his getaway with a U turn and fly out the front gate for home. If we were lucky, we rolled all the way over to the exterior wall of HQ Troop where we could use the wall to crawl up to an upright position, button up our shirt, and be ready for Retreat to be played, then somehow get one of our hands to find its way up near our forehead in order to salute when To the Colors was played. Of course, sometimes the victim just lay there until after To the Colors and we would rush them inside, hopefully, before anyone noticed.

The worst part of all this is the next day, things are still swirling around, and its hard to put one foot in front of the other, but the thing that stings the most is that queasy greasy feeling that you've been some place that you will never ever be able to completely wash off no matter how hard you scrub.

I only begin to feel a little better about all this when one day I catch a glimpse of Jacinto's GOM. It's only a momentary peek, but I'm certain he has four oak leaf clusters, which I might expect from Jacinto, but this revelation only makes me wonder how many oak leafs might the Cowboy have?

11

THE GROUND
SURVEILLANCE OFFICER

OLD TIME SERGEANTS, career sergeants, are the backbone of the military. All the knowledge, the leadership, the courage, the sacrifice is stored up here in these dedicated and knowledgeable individuals. We, all of us, owe a great deal to them. These people are the glue that holds the ranks together, the esprit in the esprit de corps, the living, breathing extension of all the sacred traditions of the United States Army.

That said, there is a misplaced loyalty in the United States Army, a fabricated device designed to extend the service of these individuals beyond a reasonable length of time. The Army accomplishes this by improvising an amendment to the regs [the Army regulations] called a 'Medical Profile' exemption.

A Medical Profile exemption is a license to let an individual who has some physical deficiency to remain on active duty out of necessity for qualified personnel, or out of a desperate need to keep them off the streets for a time for their own benefit. For all practical purposes, they can stay for as long as they care to grace us with their presence. In other words, this amendment allows them to hang around until they choose to retire.

These exemptions include things like, not requiring someone to wear boots, or tuck in their shirt, or blouse their pants [tuck in, or fold under an elastic band, their pants at the boot line] or keep the saliva in their mouth, or actually have warm blood, and the oxygen doesn't necessarily have to make it all the way up to their brain all day long.

While this may be an admirable and compassionate position, there are consequences to this particular amendment, and surprisingly a remarkable amount of hilarity may be involved.

Take, for example, Sergeant Duffy, who because of a skin condition of some severe degree, and because the army does not produce any silk rendition of the uniform, was given an exemption from even wearing a uniform. The unexpected outcome is that everyone just ignores him, it's like he isn't here. No one listens to Sergeant Duffy, he is just another civilian walking around in his pajamas, and no one has to obey a civilian in pajamas, or do we?

Or, there is the case of Sergeant Philmore, and Sergeant Bennington. After serving too long in that branch of the army that makes the most noise, the Artillery, neither one of them could hear much. If you had to address one of them, or respond to any question they may ask, you have to shout at the top of your lungs, the correct response, or the answer to their question. This, of course, leaves too much opportunity for some of us who just cannot help ourselves. When we talk to them, we intermittently cut off the volume and just move our lips until they got closer and closer then we turn it on again. This also leads to a kind of deafening of everyone around us, and increasingly the number of people on a Medical Profile for hearing deficiency continues to grow.

Often, these sergeants are given tasks that require little or no initiative or effort to accomplish. One such duty is, The Ground Surveillance Officer. The designated Ground Surveillance Officer's duty is to report any sighting of any known or unknown aircraft up the chain of command to regimental headquarters. There is a reason for this.

Both Germany and Berlin are divided up into sectors, not just the American sector, or the British sector, or the Russian sector, but there are also restricted sectors within these areas. Sectors designated as restricted sectors are delineated on maps made available to NATO and to all nations who may have representatives, diplomatic or otherwise, assigned to duties in West Germany or West Berlin. We just don't want them to know what we're up to. Countries such as the Warsaw Pact nations who have representatives in West Germany or West Berlin are forbidden to enter restricted sectors, travel through restricted sectors, or fly over restricted sectors. Yes, this really is the truth, I know it may sound incomprehensible, but some things in the military are beyond reason.

So, suppose you're a nineteen to twenty year old American trooper with plenty of time on your hands, with no real mentally taxing issues that occupy your mind, and suppose that with all this time and boredom, you need to find ways to entertain yourself and your friends, or at least, find amusing things to do with all that youth and energy.

We fall out for the Morning Formation one day, and after the head count and the usual Repair & Utilities duty is taken care of, Sergeant Willis, instead of dismissing us for our regular duties, takes this opportunity to announce to us that he has been designated as the Ground Surveillance Officer for Headquarters Troop of the 3rd Reconnaissance Squadron, 2nd Armored Cavalry Regiment, congratulations all around.

Dave whispers to T. J., "Why does a Ground Surveillance Officer always feel so good about going to work?"

T.J. responds, "I don't know, why does a Ground Surveillance Officer always feel so good about going to work?

"Because things are always looking up?"

Sergeant Willis spends about ten minutes explaining the intricacies of Ground Surveillance, restricted sectors, the Red Menace, the Iron Curtain, the Warsaw Pact, the frightening aspect of nuclear war, and the weather. Then, he enlists our assistance in fulfilling this mission to the best of our combined abilities. After that, we go off to work and no one gives another thought to the particulars of Ground Surveillance, except for T. J.

The very next morning, when Sergeant Willis steps up and asks us as a group if anyone has observed any known or unknown aircraft. T.J. steps forward, and says he believes he spotted a B One RD this morning on his way to the Mess Hall.

At first, this does not register with Sergeant Willis, he just says, "Good work, Specialist. Thanks." Then, without warning, the words somehow make it through the maze of Sergeant Willis 'mind, and he searches himself for his note pad and pencil. He fumbles around, gets flustered, dismisses everyone but T. J., and when he finds his pad and pencil, he asks T.J. for the details.

We all kind of hang around to hear this, "Well, Sarge, I believe it was one of those low flying observation aircraft with a short wing span, and a fixed landing gear...."

While T.J. is talking Sergeant Willis is writing all this down. His excitement is extremely obvious, his hands shake a little as he writes, and we guess, his breath is so shallow, and quickened by the thought of actually having something to report, he gets himself a little frazzled. He sends T.J. off to work and we see him running toward the PAL-CRYPTO room to make his report. According to the guys in PAL-CRYPTO, the Sarge actually sent a twix [a coded message] to regiment reporting the sighting of a B-1 RD.

The amazing thing is, nothing happens. No regimental response, no mention of the Sarge's success, nothing. In all probability, the guys at regiment got a kick out of it and posted it on their bulletin board and that was it. We couldn't believe this and we were so disappointed that T.J.'s little joke went nowhere.

A couple of weeks later, chagrined by the lack of any response and embolden by that same idea, T.J. carries it to the next level. Also, the Sarge's discouragement was even beginning to show up in his actions, and we wanted to reignite his enthusiasm…, well, okay, okay, we just wanted to do it again, that's all.

Sergeant Willis didn't even remember to ask about any known or unknown aircraft that morning, he just tried to dismiss us, but T.J. went for it anyway, "Sarge, Sarge, I saw a GU Eleven yesterday afternoon. This caught the Sarge off guard, and he went into his frantic pad and pencil hunting routine and when he couldn't find them, he dismissed us, and took T. J. over to the PAL-CRYPTO room to report the sighting.

The twix went out in seconds, and within minutes the response came back.

"ZZZZDDDXRAY$%^%%$$0830HRS2208196819 68**2ACR2ACR****GROUNDSURVEILLANCEREP ORT3DSQDN***REPEAT2ACR2ACRGROUNDSURV EILLANCEREPORT3DSQDN**ATTENTIONATTEN TION**CEASEDESISTCEASEDESIST***BYORDERO FCOMMANDERRELIEVEGROUNDSURVEILLANCE OFFICER**CEASEDESISTCEASEDESIST**REMOVE GROUNDSURVEILLANCEOFFICER***SUSPENDGR OUNDSURVEILLANCEREPORTINGUNTILFURTHE RNOTICEZZZZDDDXRAY$%^%%$$0830HRS220819 68**1968**2ACR2ACR***GROUNDSURVEILLANCE REPORT3DSQDN***REPEAT2ACR2ACRGROUNDS

URVEILLANCEREPORT3DSQDN****ATTENTIONA
TTENTION**CEASEDESISTCEASEDESIST******BY
ORDEROFCOMMANDER***RELIEVEGROUNDSUR
VEILLANCEOFFICER**CEASEDESISTCEASEDESIS
T**RELIEVEGROUNDSURVEILLANCEOFFICER***
*******SUSPENDGROUNDSURVEILLANCEREPOR
TINGUNTILFURTHERNOTICE*******ZZZZDDDX
RAY$%^%%$$0830HRS220819681968."

Sergeant Willis, after his honorable service of thirty-six years took his full retirement from active duty. And, when we were processing him out of the 3rd Herd for rotation back stateside for retirement, he pulled T.J. aside and thanked him.

12

SHIRLEY TEMPLE & THE SOVIET INVASION OF CZECHOSLOVAKIA

IT WAS A Tuesday, and for some reason unknown to me, we met Jacinto, Dave and Pete at the Ring Café, then we spent several hours in the hooting, hollering and drinking section of Amberg, in and around the Ranch Bar. Things were pretty slow that night, not slow enough to keep us sober, but slow enough, so we headed for the Pond about ten.

T.J. tried to lie down on a bench in the moat, but Jacinto and Pete got him up, and we managed to climb the hill up to the Pond. I remember, everyone grousing about how dull this place is, and how we should go to Nurnberg next weekend. As we hit the sack, the alert sirens went off, and everyone kind of groaned and turned over in bed, but no one bothered to get up.

Then we heard a bunch of racket in the hallway and Sergeant Cibolo threw the door to our room open, and as "Good Lovin'" blared out of the speakers, Cibolo yelled, "GET YOUR SAD SACK ASSES OUT OF BED! THIS IS WAR!"

"Dave looked up, and said, "Oh, my gawd, Sergeant T. Totaler is drunk, someone write that down."

For some reason the sirens kept going off long after someone should have turned them off, and out of the blue, Sergeant Green shows up. The First Sergeant, himself, is standing there yelling, so we know something is up, we just don't know what. "GET UP! GET UP! GET YOUR GEAR! GET UP! GET OUT TO THE MOTOR STABLES! NOW! NOW! DO IT NOW!"

When we got down to the armory to draw our weapons, Zieglar, the Armorer issued our rifles, and told us the C.O. of I Troop had taken our .50 caliber machine gun, which was a great relief to us because none of us wanted to lug that hunk of metal around with us all night anyway.

As we straggled along over toward the office to get the coffee going, and print some more notices, Sergeant Tyler ran up the walk and told us to go report to Sergeant Solomon in the Motor Stables. Pete asked, "What about the NEO?" Sergeant T. laughed and said, "It's too bad for them, they're on their own for this one," and he trotted off toward the Head Shed. Now, we knew something was up, but we didn't have a clue what exactly it was.

Things were getting crazy out in the Motor Stables, Sergeant Solomon looked haggard, and excited at the same time and he put us on a deuce and half, and said,

"Good Luck, boys. Give 'em hell," or something like that, and we rolled out the main gate with the real troopers, a bunch of guys from I Troop.

The old rumor mill was churning and someone said the Russians crossed the border and we were at war. Some clown says, "Anybody got an extra clip on them?" and some other guy says, "You don't need another clip, in few minutes you're just gonna be a greasy spot on the highway." All I could think was, this couldn't be right, they would have already bombed us, and just as I thought this, several jets screamed overhead, and I ducked and everyone laughed.

For some reason, I thought about the S.T.A.G.G. board and how we forgot it, and who would update it tomorrow, and if something happened to Lombardo, or whoever it was that was on the bottom, who might take his place because I can't remember who is on the next line above Lombardo, but I need to tell them.

When we get up to the border, the West Germans are no where to be seen, [usually they are up there a few meters in front of us on the wire, but no one sees them], and then they come along and move us up to the positions the West Germans usually take and Roy looks up at the border and it's not a good sign, he says that the 12th Panzers have torn through the border fences, plowed up the ground, and gone into Czechoslovakia.

I see Galardo, the Commo Sergeant, running along with a reel of wire, and he goes into a tempo- rary O.P.[Observation Post] and disappears. I look at Jacinto, and he looks back at me and we try to laugh, but neither one of us can.

"Dig in, dig in," a voice yells from the darkness, and we start looking for our entrenching tools, I don't usually bring mine to alerts, but I accidentally did this time. It's so dark, I can't see much, but I start digging, and Jacinto yells at me to turn around and quit throwing dirt at him.

Finally, Sergeant Tyler shows up and tells us the Russians invaded Czechoslovakia last night and N.A.T.O. is trying to figure out whether to assist the Czechs or not. The XO comes along and tells George, the 3d Herd is going to be here a while, and he tells him to get his guys and start hauling ammo and rations up from the Pond to the border.

The Sergeant gets all of us together and he gets a couple of trucks off K Troop, and we head back to Amberg. The celebration starts as soon as we are out of earshot of the border.

While everyone else sits up there on the edge of their seat waiting for the Russkies to attack, we hump ammo all night, and then cases and cases of C Rations and K Rations. In the early morning, on our last run back up to the border, Billy Wayne blows a tire and we swerve off the road, Roy and I start looking for the Sirens of the Oberpfalz but it's just wishful thinking.

We can't go anywhere so we just sit there, eating from our cache of rations. Finally, a mechanic shows up and we hitch a ride with a friend of Billy Wayne back up to the border with another load of ammo and rations. This time they send us all the up to the Waidhaus border crossing. As we get close to the border thousands of people are coming across from Czechoslovakia, they mob our truck and we have to fight them off. An officer fires off a couple of rounds in the air, and they settle down. When I turn around I see the officer is our Adjutant, LT MIke. He organizes the distribution of the rations, and we hump the ammo over to a bunker.

By this time most of us are sober, but so ragged out we can hardly move. Sergeant Tyler tells us the West Germans are coming out of Czechoslovakia.

Then, just as we get comfortable, an arrogant little major comes along tells George to get all of us over into the Medical tent that is set up just off the road. We wait here for an hour, then this arrogant little munchkin major comes back and tells everyone to shut up, then he starts his speech.

"Good Afternoon, troopers. My name is Major Pomeroy. I am an Intelligence Officer from G-2 at VII Corps [which explains a lot]. This debriefing is less about what you have observed over the last few hours, and more about what you will be able to share about what you observed over the next few decades."

"Before you leave this facility today, you will sign a debriefing statement agreeing to abide by the directives of this statement. You may choose not to sign this debriefing statement, however, if you refuse to sign and abide by the directives laid out in this debriefing, you will immediately be taken into custody until such time as you can agree to abide by this directive. In essence, this directive states that you and your unit, ah, ah, uh, oh, the 3d Reconnaissance Squadron of the 2d Armored Cavalry Regiment did on or about 1155 hours on 20 August 1968 participate in a NATO alert, involving the rapid response deployment of your unit to your customary positions near the Czechoslovakian border. At 0900 hours on 21 August 1968 this alert was deemed accomplished. Further, at no time during this period did you observe any units of the Federal Republic of Germany [the Bundeswehr] encroach, enter, violate, or cross the international border designated as the Federal Republic of Germany/Czechoslovakia border. Nor did you observe any units of the Federal Republic of Germany [the Bundeswehr] re-enter the Federal Republic of Germany from any adjacent border. Upon my honor as a sworn member of the United States Armed Forces."

"Questions? Good. My assistants are at this time passing out these debriefing statements, please sign in the appropriate space, exchange your statement with the individual next to you, witness his statement, and pass the forms back to the front. Questions? Good. Proceed."

I signed my statement, Marilyn Monroe, gave it to Jacinto, he handed me his, he had signed his John Lennon, so we witnessed each other's statements and passed them forward.

When we got back outside, a crowd was gathering around some disheveled woman being mobbed by the press and a bunch of G.I.s. I ask a medic who she was, "Yeah, I think that's Shirley Temple, the former child movie star. Apparently, she's a United States ambassador now. Someone says she was in Prague when the Russkies attacked. They got her out somehow."

I looked over there at Miss Temple and thought she looked like a grown up Heidi, but she seemed to be having trouble getting her grumpy to turn back into cuddly this time.

13

COLD WAR BRIDES

HERE'S A MYSTERY that baffles masculine curiosity, and its never been logically explained to anyone's satisfaction.

Why would any young, beautiful, sane, American woman want to forsake all the fun and opportunity available to her in the good old U. S. of A., leave her family and friends behind, travel thousands of miles at her own expense to live in a foreign country that speaks a language she does not understand, live on a meager income in a little tiny apartment, with no car, and nothing to do with herself for up to 16 hours a day for months, if not years, on end.

And, everything else aside, why, at the same time, would she want to put up with an immature, irresponsible guy with such an exaggerated sense of patriotism that he has, for some inexplicable reason, joined the Army [in the midst of the Free Love/Vietnam Era], and has accumulated a cadre of very freaky friends who don't want to do anything but drink and carouse around the countryside looking for girls and castles and/or another Gasthaus?

Sounds crazy, right? We don't get it either, but we saw this with our own eyes, and it still makes us wonder, especially, at such a young age, at this particular time of our lives, in the middle of this, our great and wonderful, once in a lifetime, soldier of fortune international adventure of passion, intrigue and hedonism, why would anyone throw caution to the wind like this?

Two of our own number showed up here with a wife [not the same one, of course, but one each], and that's pretty ordinary. I mean, people are able to accept this, you know, they are married, they have made promises, they are making the noble sacrifice and all that kind of stuff.

But, how could someone actually do this on purpose. It leads us to believe that something is askew, someone may not be playing with a full deck, or someone may be under the spell of some malevolent scheme to lure an innocent into a web of intrigue with less than honorable intentions, which we suspected, but could not prove.

It was only after completing our rigorous tests of, 1-determining the mental stability of our friends, Eddy and Roy, and 2-being assured there was no plot or conspiracy afoot to take advantage of some innocent girl. And in our review, we learn, quite by accident, that the motive behind all this getting married stuff might actually be valid, but we also learn it takes a remarkable amount of supplication to convince someone to do this. Finally, it all came down to this simple, quite human expression of emotion, exercised and accomplished with superior skill and cunning by our friends, Eddy and Roy—they both relied on the abject fear of failure, along with mucho begging, pleading, groveling, bribery, and various exaggerated coercions, not to mention prayer and veiled threats of self destructive behaviors to overwhelm the compassion of their intendeds, Patricia and Gail, and without reason-they accepted.

Once all the investigations, and begging and stuff are over with, it finally occurs to the 'boys' that in order to pull off something like this it might take more than just supplication and acceptance to get this thing off the ground. So, finding themselves one conspiracy short of a victory, they go looking for help.

Both Eddy and Roy figure it's times like these your buddies need to step up and fulfill their commitment to the certain obligations of friendship that they signed up for when they borrowed your civvies to go on leave, your last dollar, your ration card, ask you to fill in for them on the trash detail, or the Duty Clerk jobs. And, of course, you know they will, just like the time they left you downtown on a park bench when it started snowing because you got so wasted you couldn't walk [just to teach you a lesson you could understand], and not to forget the time they gave you that Bundeswehr Officer's hat and overcoat they lifted off the coat rack in that Gasthaus downtown and went sporting around in the Ranch Bar until just before the Polizei showed up, and they gave it to you, or the many times they stole the key to the Chapel door that gives access through the perimeter wall of the Pond long after all those Cinderella passes of yours had expired and you were, in effect, AWOL, and out in the cold, so to speak [literally], until you agreed to pay the requisite fee to get back inside.

Luckily, for one Eddy P. [not his real name], and one Roy P. [not his real name], they had the kind of friends you can count on when the chips are down, your back's to the wall, your guts are in a knot, and you don't what to do next.

And, it takes friends like these, friends like Merlin to make things happen. I don't know how old Merlin is, I never asked him, and he never offered to tell me. I just know he was ageless then, and he's probably ageless now. Merlin looks like your average mysterious stranger. Another thing is, he drives a big black Mercedes. How does an American G.I. drive a big black Mercedes? The same way anyone else does, but they don't look as cool as Merlin does in his. He looks at his car sometimes, and he turns around to see who's watching and he screams it aloud, "Das Beste Oder Nichts'.

I see him sometimes outside in the sunshine, I don't know where he is the rest of the time; I don't think anyone else does either. I see him walking toward the back parking lot near the old Pershing tank, coming out of the Class Six store, carrying a heavy package. He has his smooth black leather jacket on; his motorcycle boots; his black hair and deep dark eyes make a stark transition to his pale face, his ruddy complexion. Merlin has an unmistakable presence that he carries around with him, a kind of foreboding look, until he smiles, or he laughs and all that collapses into another Merlin. I like both of them. Merlin solves all the transportation problems for the wedding party.

Sally [Olin's bride], on the other hand, is the essence of sweetness and light. I'm going to say, petite, because I know she doesn't like to be called cute, and I don't know how else to say it. Everyone likes Sally without even trying. I think I know why. Sally knows how to do things, she knows how things work, not just mechanical things, but the people things, too, the important, yet ordinary everyday things that make life work pretty smoothly without too many complications, which we seem to run into a lot since we've been over here on our own without a clue, so to speak. I think she's a nurse or something like that in real life, and she's the first actual 'lady' I've ever known besides my mom. Don't tell Sally I said this, because I don't think she likes that word 'lady' much either.

As it turns out, Olin and Sally are the only adults here, at least, the only ones in our group, but they manage somehow to keep up their disguise as our friends without us even realizing it until we have to. This is a good thing for us, we may not admit this to anyone, but we all know this, and we have come to appreciate the great good fortune of having Olin and Sally friends. Olin and Sally solve all the secular paperwork problems and provide the venue for the wedding reception.

The first to get hitched, Eddy and Pat. Pat, after months of research and document reproduction [the Catholic bureaucracy needs to know], packed her bags and headed for Frankfurt with this one singular resolution, if Eddy was not there at the airport, she had booked her return on the next flight out. Eddy was there.

After declining the opportunity of getting married in the Consolidated Mess Hall, Pat, with the help of Sally, Olin, Merlin, and Fred and Oochie [the German couple who invited Eddy to Christmas Dinner, and now have helped secure access to the church, Mariahilfberg, and walked Pat and Eddy through the civil marriage maze [a consequence of getting married in Germany]. They had connections down at the Burgermeister's office. The next day, Merlin delivered the Patricia to the summit of the highest hill near Amberg [a pretty steep climb] in the big black Mercedes to Mariahilfberg, a beautiful [really a storybook kind of place] Franciscan monastery and church overlooking Amberg with an audience, mostly sober, of most of the guys from the Pond. Fred and Oochie's kids acted as ring bearer/ flower girl, and it was done.

The reception, hosted by Olin and Sally, at their place [a really fantastic contemporary apartment] made us look like we knew what we were doing.

Months later, Gail found her way to the Pond, and Gail and Roy, with the same cadre of assistants worked their magic on the bureaucracy of church and state. And, when Eddy P. volunteered to do the music for the church wedding everything seemed to fall into place.

Then, Roy and Eddy went up to Mariahilfberg to take a look at the organ and after some furtive attempts at making music with this ancient instrument, they decided to hire someone who really knew what they were doing.

The reception at Gail and Roy's apartment, 16 Uhlandstrasse [which means 'upland' or 'crash land', we're not sure which], but it lived up to one or both of its names depending on whom you believe.

As it turns out, the Champagne Cork firing competition, gave Gail and Roy a less than enthusiastic introduction to their German neighbors [the Polzei only showed up afterwards], and at the height of the celebrations, in keeping with the great American tradition of mischievous wedding pranks, all the labels on the canned goods in the pantry disappeared, and by some mysterious spell of balance and levitation, their bed remained precariously connected to the earth somehow over the months they lived there on Uhlandstrasse without collapsing under the stress of marital bliss.

All and all, these two events [four if your counting civil and spiritual] made a lasting impression on us for all the obvious reasons, and some other inexplicable ones.

As it turns out these two girls, Gail and Pat, brought us some measure of hearth and home to our overseas military lives, and reminded us of our connection to the real world that we would one day maybe have to find our way back to. So, in the interim, this whole thing, aside from the obvious benefits to the principals, made a significant contribution to the way we were then, and the way we see things today, because of our girls who brought us a home away from home, so to speak.

After the initial trauma and shock of meeting us, Gail fit right in. She may have often wondered how she got here, but I don't believe she ever missed a moment of the fun. She was always there to make it seem like this extraordinary time would last forever, and it has.

Without really doing, or saying anything, Pat holds us up to the standard she sets for us, and without really trying it works like magic on us. This is really strange, just one look, and suddenly we want to be what she wants us to be. We may not necessarily want to be responsible, but somehow this is the only option we have when Pat's around.

Cold War Brides? We have to say, we like the concept and love the outcome.

14

RAINCOAT PROMOTIONS

A PERSONNEL SPECIALIST is given the MOS [Military Occupational Specialty] of 71H20, the United States Army's definition of a clerk. Becoming a clerk in a personnel office in the United States Army is like being made a General without the pay grade, but with much more responsibility, and much less pomp and circumstance, and it's a whole lot more fun.

Truth be told, it's the personnel in the Personnel Office, not the Generals, who run the Army. Personnel Specialists make all the promotions, all the personnel evaluations, all the pay changes, we cut all the orders, we handle the reenlistments and the discharges, the early releases from active duty, and we make sure everyone serves their bad time [bad time is the time you must serve to make up for any time you spend in civilian or military custody because you were bad, in effect your enlistment or draft time stops upon your incarceration, and continues only after your release]. Of course, if you have bad time to serve, your active duty service is not your most pressing obligation.

Personnel assigns everyone to a particular slot on the T. O. & E., we record all the leave dates, award all the medals, we send people home, and we send them off to other commands, we record the Article 15s and the Courts Martial, we escort people to the stockade, and release them from the stockade, we make sure everyone is paid, or not paid, and we document their medical profiles, we send people out on TDY [Temporary Duty], and we bring them back, and on and on. In fact, you only actually exist, if someone in personnel says you exist. The only position in the United States Army with more sway over the daily lives of each and every soldier is the Mail Clerk, the highest ranking position in the United States Armed Forces.

All this personnel stuff is accomplished simply by employing the various rules and regulations outlined in a series of regulations beginning with AR 600-8 [Army Regulation 600-8] through and inclusive of AR 635-200. All the magic happens here, and all the ways to make the magic is explained here.

In all of our time in Germany, we only had one singular officer with the mental capacity to put all this together, and he is the only one with the presence of mind to ask, out loud, the questions no other officer wanted to know the answer to, and we never really knew for sure if he knew what he was asking or if he just wanted to keep us on our best behavior. Lt. Mike was not a career officer. He became an officer through

OCS, [Officer Candidate School [or, a ninety day wonder as the saying goes].

The main thing here is, he was just like us, serving his time and aching to get back to being a civilian. He made no bones about this, and we all respected him for this, because if an officer does this openly he never will get promoted by the good old boy West Point network no matter what he is capable of, or actually accomplishes.

Lt. Mike, the Adjutant of the 3rd Reconnaissance Squadron, was often in our offices fulfilling the obligations of an Adjutant [reviewing the T. O. & E., reviewing all the orders issued by the Personnel Office because at the bottom of each order it reads: FOR THE COMMANDER: [the signature of the Adjutant] and his signature block Michael D., 1st Lt., Adjutant.

At first, he made as diligent an effort as anyone could have expected of an Adjutant, but as time went on, Lt. Mike decided that the less he actually knew about what went on in the Personnel Office the better off he might be, and his visits became less and less frequent. However, LT never lost his edge, and he would walk into the office and actually say things out loud that would surprise us and often make us scramble for an explanation. This is why we liked him so much, almost any explanation would do, because as often as not, he knew what he was asking, he just liked to see us squirm. Our guess is, when you're as smart as LT you just can't help yourself. It's just too much fun to twist the tail of the dragoon.

LT stumbles into Personnel one day, the day William Merrifield is rotating back to the world. He stops in his tracks, he looks at Jacinto, he looks at Merrifield, he looks at his watch, he stares off into the distance a moment, and without any expression at all to let us know he is kidding us again, he asks, "Why do so many guys in this outfit always leave here in a Raincoat, and it never is raining?" [of course, this is because their friendship with us in personnel has won them one unauthorized promotion to the next highest rank as they rotate home, and the raincoat hides their new stripes].

The place went semi-silent for a second, then someone giggled. No one moved. There was a heavy scent of fear in the room. LT looked at us, made us think about his question, and with a big grin on his face, he immediately turned himself around, and with a mumbled, "As you were..." he left the room.

We grabbed up Merrifield's stuff, and hustled him off the post and down to the Bahnhof, had a few drinks and sent him on his way home.

LT never quit asking all the right questions, and I think he always read the orders we published with a tongue in his cheek sort of smile on his face, but he kept a close eye on the T. O. & E., and when he did come into the Personnel Office he liked to pick his target and look over their shoulder long enough to make us uncomfortable enough to know we weren't fooling anyone but ourselves. So, when it came time to say good-bye to LT, everyone was pretty upset that he was going. We wanted to show our appreciation for his forbearance on our behalf, so we did the right thing. Rather than ask him if he wanted to or not, we just pitched in, bought him and raincoat, and we gave him two sets of personnel records [one set sent him home an LT, the other set sent him home as a recently promoted Captain, his choice], and Olin dropped his Captain's bars into the pocket of his raincoat.

15

THE EXTRA DUTY ROSTER

THE THING IS, in this strict order, you never want to mess with the Mail Clerk, the Personnel Specialist, the Cook, or a General. If you do, there are consequences.

The Extra Duty Roster is produced by the First Sergeant of Headquarters Troop. The Extra Duty Roster assigns individuals to certain duties over the course of the week that are not permanent duties, but duties shared by everyone in the unit. These assignments include: KP [Kitchen Police], Guard Duty [the Ammo Dump, the Airfield, the Post], etc.

The Personnel Section, due to their critical and essential work in the ongoing effectiveness of the unit is exempt from the Extra Duty Roster in most cases for obvious reasons.

Unfortunately, our First Sergeant, First Sergeant Archibald Green decided to include the Personnel staff on the Extra Duty Roster without consulting the Personnel Sergeant. At first, we thought this was a joke, or an easily correctable mistake, but certainly an error of some kind. As it turns out it was an error, an error in judgment by the First Sergeant.

Ignoring all the obvious warnings and comments by Sergeant Tyler, Archibald proceeded with his plan, and refused to remove the Personnel Office staff from the Extra Duty Roster.

The next day with no other alternative, a certain Personnel Specialist called 14th Finance Section in Nurnberg to see why First Sergeant Green's pay records were missing. 14th Finance reported that First Sergeant Green's pay records must have been misplaced somehow, it seems like the Pay records for one First Sergeant Archie Green might be missing until further notice.

Pay Day was the Thursday after the Personnel Section was put on the Extra Duty roster. Sergeant Green showed up in the Personnel Office shortly after Pay Call explaining that he had not received his monthly pay. Of course, we sympathized with the Sergeant, but we had to tell him that as soon as the Personnel Payroll Clerk returned to duty after pulling guard all night, we would get right on it. This did not register with Sergeant Green, he looked a little frustrated and discouraged, grumbled under his breath, then he asked if there was anything we could do in the meantime. Specialist Cannon jumped up and said, "Yes, yes Sergeant. Please sit down here, and let me process a partial payment for you until this is all straightened out."

Sergeant Green smiled and said, "Well, that's great Specialist." And, he was happy for a moment as he answered Specialist Cannon's questions, then he asked, "How much of a partial payment can I get today?"

And, Cannon had to tell him, "We can get you twenty-five dollars here by Monday or Tuesday, maybe."

On Monday, a new Extra Duty Roster was issued by the First Sergeant of Headquarters Troop. No one from the Personnel Office appeared on the Extra Duty Roster. Problem solved.

We thought, but we only thought this until Archie's pay showed up the following week, and on the following Monday, the new Extra Duty Roster appeared with half of the Personnel Office staff on KP and the other half on Guard Duty. No complaints from the Personnel Section, we just waited in anticipation of the next Pay Day.

Sergeant Green shows up again just after Pay Call, it seems that somehow his pay records were missing from 14th Finance again, and he was again, not paid. There was a mausoleum quality silence in the Personnel Office as Cannon filled out the Partial Pay Request. The Sergeant kept trying to figure out what to say to us, but there just weren't any words to describe his anger, and he wasn't about to let us get the best of him. He went directly to our Sergeant Tyler after hours.

"I know what's going on here, Tyler." Archibald was gritting his teeth.

"Yeah," George said, "so do I."

This surprised Arch, "You telling me you know, and you're letting them do this to me."

George smiled, "What I know, is that we can't keep a Personnel Office running efficiently when we have people traipsing around at all hours of the night out at the ammo dump, or have people mopping floors in the Mess Hall, things go undone when you keep my people away, they can't do their jobs, but we'll manage as best we can, even if sometimes we can't get it all done at once."

"I'm gonna...gonna... remember this, George."

"Please do, Arch, that's the most important part of the learning process."

The Personnel Office staff was removed from the Extra Duty Roster, forever.

*[Anecdotal evidence of Karma: After his release from active duty, Jack and his Dad went down to Fort Hood to enter the drawing for the privilege of deer hunting on Fort Hood property. As Jack was filling out his form for the drawing, a Sergeant sidled up next to him and asked, "What are doing there Trooper?" Without looking up Jack told the guy, "Oh, just filling out the form for the drawing," then with the sting of recognition in the sound of a voice out of his past, Jack looked up. Sergeant Archie Green was standing there, he smiled, and said, "Ya know, I have this suspicion your name will not be drawn today."]

16

LOST & FOUND IN A REFORGER

THE ACTUAL CONCEPT was to reduce the USAREUR force by a few divisions while in the same breath reassuring our N.A.T. O. allies that this reduction of forces could be done without jeopardizing the critical defenses of Western Europe, and at the same time, showing the Russkies that just because we might be willing to jeopardize the critical defenses of Western Europe, this really didn't mean that we were willing to do this in plain view of the Iron Curtain without acting like this was no big deal, and we could probably bring all these forces back from the USA within a moments notice of any real or perceived Warsaw Pact threat any time we felt like it. And, just to prove that this classic mistake was for real, the Reforger exercise was initiated and held every year from 1969 to 1993, except for a couple of odd years when the walls came tumbling down and the old Iron Curtain rusted through.

This is why I think the whole idea for this REFORGER [RE turn FOR ces to GER many] thing had less to do with economic, strategic or tactical issues, and more to do with some solitary soul deep down in the dark recesses of the Pentagon who was embarrassed about this unprecedented reduction in force, if not bored to tears and desperate for any kind of excitement at all, tragic or comic, and it probably went something like this,

General Reston McKeister may have said something like this to his staff, "Hey kids, why don't we get everyone together and put on a big show!"

This massive exercise involved moving thousands and thousands of pieces of equipment and personnel, over thousands and thousands of miles, dropping them into a staging area, and giving them a sometimes complete, sometimes incomplete set of maps, and wishing them well, and telling them the defense of the free world rested on their shoulders, and then setting off the sirens that initiated a joint USAREUR/N.A.T.O. training exercise that often lost its way in the Oberpfalz.

This Reforger game put experienced allied units stationed in Germany and familiar with the terrain, combat tactics, all the good hiding places, and with a practiced knowledge of where to find a gasthaus or a beer garden when you need one, up against an often inexperienced, disoriented force flown in from the States and composed of a mixture of partly active, partly reserve units, under/over supplied with vehicles, equipment, and tactics that did not necessarily match their objectives, and often left them wondering why they were so cold, dirty, and hungry on this, their first ever, European vacation.

Reforger did accomplish this one singular thing in its many fits and starts. Reforger gave rise to the greatest strength of the United States Armed Forces and reinforced the inherent ability of our troops to improvise, adapt, and overcome in order to achieve an objective. And, this ability was expressed in many phenomenal and ancillary innovations inspired by these war games that, I believe, did actually make it a great success in spite of its shaky origins.

For the most part these great successes grew out of the very circumstances of these same War Games, like for instance one of our favorites-GOFILOREOFF [GO FInd LOst REforger OFFicers]. Note: Each of our maneuvers took the name and shape we designed for it based on our original guiding compression of the words used to create the name Reforger, itself.

When all of these units arrived in Germany at once, there had to be some minor set backs and confusion. The maps issued to these units were accurate graphic representations of the earth's surface drawn to scale, and assembled in a set of map sheets, which required more than a passing familiarity with the critical processes of land navigation. A constant aggravation to these Reforger troops was trying to determine exactly which map sheet they were on and which map sheets did they actually need in order to get to where they wanted to or were supposed to go.

This obviously led to some innovative and inspired manipulation of these maps. Many Reforger Officers in the field took to carefully taping the map sheets together. This not only required the requisite amount of spatial ability, but also an infinite, even monastic amount of patience and faith. And, very often even this laborious undertaking did not exactly help the situation, because some of these maps were not exactly put together correctly, sequentially speaking, and the comedy involved when folding and/or unfolding the same to the full extent needed to find out where they might be, or where they might go, rivaled, no surpassed, any vacationers nightmare of trying to get the complimentary Texaco US Interstate map back into or out of the glove box.

When the frustration, hunger, fuel and desperation finally set in and/or ran out, some of these lost units called for assistance, and we would dutifully go out and find them and put them back on the road to recovery of their dignity, if not their objective.

A corollary maneuver to the GOFILOREOFF was the GOFIREUNRUGA [GO FInd REforger UNits who have RUn out of GAs] which very often related more to the map folding skills of the Reforger officer than any fuel consumption issue. And, against all odds GOFIREUNRUGA became a ubiquitous and hilarious pastime we enjoyed for the challenge as much as for the comic relief it offered. GOFIREUNRUGA officers less burdened by the human condition, and willing to ask for help often fared much better than the unfortunate few who were unwilling to stop and get directions.

The more serious complications of this whole Reforger spectrum of problems involved the initial distribution of supplies and equipment. While some units greatly benefited from the experience and skill of their S-4 [Supply/Quartermaster] Noncommissioned Officers, others suffered the dire consequences of being understaffed in this critical military occupational specialty.

A case in point, while several components of the same training force might find themselves with 32,000 rolls of toilet paper, their counterparts in another unit might experience a complete, unfortunate, and desperate lack of a single square. An issue of this nature led to the improvisation of an assembly of Emergency Response Units of the RETPAREUNWO [REpatriate Toilet PAper to REforger UNits WithOut] maneuver. All of the Emergency units were kept on high alert to provide an immediate response to these critical shortages, and were put on a roving grid throughout the Hohenfels Training Area.

In the aftermath of the first and the many subsequent Reforger exercises an unexpected consequence of these war games reared its ugly head toward the end of each Reforger. This issue gave rise to the COMGERFARTOCRO [COMpensate GERman FARmers for TOrn up CROps] maneuver. The COMGERFARTOCRO can trace its sordid origins back to the 'map in the glove box' dilemma of our initial concern. But, the fact is, a 52 ton main battle tank [the M60A1] up to and including the 60 ton M1A1 can do a remarkable amount of damage to a field under cultivation, and as many of us might suspect, these tracked vehicles, even with the customary road pads installed, can undo in a few minutes what might take a whole season of plow, plant, grow and reap to accomplish. So, inevitably some of our 'lost' units strayed out of bounds of the training area and found themselves waist deep in the green of a German farmers livelihood. So, following each Reforger we spent a good deal of our time identifying, photographing, filing, and processing the complaints of German farmers concerning the loss of certain assets at the hands of the USAREUR. All resolved, of course, through the COMGERFARTOCRO Reimbursement Fund.

The most surprising derivative maneuver of any Reforger was the REGERDAUSA [REdeploy GERman DAughters to the USA] maneuver. The unintentional interactions spawned by the GOFILOREOFF, the GOFIREUNRUGA, the RETPAREUNWO the and the COMGERFARTOCRO inspired and/or aspired to an inordinate amount of sudden and hasty love connections, unexpected courtships, and the inevitable marriage of some German daughters and American servicemen caught up in the throes of another Reforger. And, the consequent personnel processing requirements of the United States Army for any military personnel's marriage to a foreign national, and the requisite processing of dependent identification forms and the updating of personnel records to expedite certain pay allowances and the rotation of once German single women, now American wives back to the United States of America and/or the obverse, the processing of European discharges for military personnel requesting same at the completion of their tour of duty kept the personality shop busy for weeks.

All in all, I'm guessing the best thing that came out of all this Reforger stuff, especially the map in the glove box folding-unfolding issue, was the discovery of the absolute necessity of a universal Global Positioning System, or more commonly known as a GPS, which without the influence, innovations and critical losses of the Reforger exercises might still be decades away.

17

RAINDROPS ON ROSES

IT WAS ON a Saturday, yeah, it was on a Saturday after months and months on the Pond. My insides felt kind of strange that morning, not strange funny, but just strange strange. I didn't notice this at first, it just slipped up from behind me and took over when I wasn't looking. I only discovered why this happened later, by accident.

I went downtown that morning, I went down there alone. I poked around the Marketplatz, I saw Adellonda. She was shopping, and I walked along with her for a while. Then we sat down and shared a strudel. There was nothing very extraordinary about this day, it was just like any other day, just like all the other days here in Amberg, except for this one startling thing. When she was leaving me I was standing there in the Marketplatz, and I said the strangest thing to her, I said, "Bis spater."

I didn't notice this at first. It's just an ordinary phrase, a common colloquialism for, 'See you later.'

Then, it hit me, all this time I was walking along with Adellonda–I was talking to her. I was actually talking to her. I was talking to her in German!

When I realized this, I turned around and I looked across the Marketplatz. I knew every building, every little nook and cranny, nothing looked foreign to me, nothing looked out of place, nothing looked unusual. I couldn't understand this at first, then all the sounds of the place swelled up around me and I could hear them, I could actually hear them, and I knew what everyone was saying. So, without really trying, without even knowing what was happening, I grasp the meaning of all this for the first time, I knew it without knowing it. I knew that I live here, I know this place, I belong here, this is my home now! The thought of it frightened me. What happened to me? When did this happen?

I ran away. I ran all the way back up to the Pond. I went to the office, but no one was there. All I knew was I needed to find my old self, my original self, and I decided that I needed to go somewhere I did not know so well, so I could do that. I needed to get out of here. I grabbed a Leave request form and filled it out, forged the necessary signatures, and took it straight over to Headquarters Troop.

When I got down to the Bahnhof the next Friday, Bill, a G. I. from Detroit was there. I asked Bill where he was going, he said Salzburg. I thought about this a minute, I had never seen Salzburg, and everyone I knew said it was a great place to take Leave. I decided to join up with Bill, and we got on the train to Salzburg via Munchen.

I really didn't know what to expect, but it was more about getting out of there, off the Pond, for while that really mattered. And, a couple of weeks ago as the projectionist at the post theater, I had shown the movie, "The Sound of Music" three times in two days. That's right all twenty-three reels of it, over and over and over. So, I felt like this might be the kind of place where I could find myself, you know, climb every mountain, ford every stream.

When the train puffed into the valley where Salzburg, Austria is, I saw a wonderful place. The Alps are within sight of this town, the Sulzach River, almost a rapid, bright blue and cold runs through it, an ancient fortress looms over it, and the architecture—take your pick—Romanesque, Gothic, Renaissance, Baroque is everywhere.

When we arrived, we went looking for the Blaue Gans [the Blue Goose], the guys back on the Pond said it was cheap and clean [a buck fifty a night]. It was full, but we got a room at the Elfant around the corner [2.50 a night], a really nice place. We were in Austria now, but I noticed the Bavarian dialect still hanging in the air, everyone sounded like they were from the Oberpfalz, nothing much seemed to have changed except the scenery.

Bill and I took off to see the sights. He said we needed to take a Gray Line tour of the town first. I looked sideways at Bill, and said, "You mean the tourist route, I don't think so."

Bill laughed at me, then he started telling me the secrets Merlin had told him just before we left. Merlin says, the best way to meet girls is to get on the Gray Line tour bus when we first get here, this way we get an overall look at the place, and we might find some young American girls to see it with, but if there aren't any girls, we're supposed to take this same tour at least a couple of times more if it's in the summer because it's almost a sure thing.

I wasn't paying much attention after the first tour, I just got back on the bus and took a seat in the row behind Bill. A bunch of old ladies got on the bus, filled up most of the seats in front of us. I was looking at a tourist map, when I heard someone say, "Enschuldigen, Sie, bitte. Ist diese Platz frei?"

I didn't look up, I just said, "Wie bitte?" There was no response, so I glanced up and saw this real live girl, and I fell over myself, saying, "Bitte, Setzen Sie sich, heir, bitte." There was a brunette behind her, she sat down next to Bill. They were both gorgeous, they may not have been American, but I suddenly thought, I don't think I want to be so choosy any more.

I attempted to introduce myself, "Guten Tag, mein namen ist Jack, und das ist mein Freund, Bill."

They both laughed, and in English they asked us in unison, "Are you Americans?"

"We are," Bill said, "Detroit," and I added, "Texas. Where are you from?"

They were from Ottawa, Ontario, Wendy [the beautiful brunette] and Bonnie [the gorgeous blonde] are Canadians. I had never met a Canadian until this very moment, and in a panic I struggled to recall all my Canadian vocabulary, but I came up with nothing.

Flush faced and desperate, I said, "I've never been to Canada, but isn't it close to Detroit." They laughed again, the ice was broken, and as we pulled away from the curb, it was Wendy and Bill, and Bonnie and Jack on the Gray Line tour of Salzburg. I reminded myself to thank Merlin, again.

We were smitten, Wendy and Bonnie were real life people with real life jobs in Ottawa, and they had saved up enough to do the European whirlwind tour thing. I kept slipping up and falling back into German sometimes, but the longer we were together the more that faded. I started to think I knew who I was again, and it felt pretty great to be speaking English, to English speaking women, and being understood at the same time.

We visited the places we all liked from our Gray Line tour, die Wasserspiele Hellbrun, Mirabell Palace & Gardens, the Fortress, a side trip to the Salt mines and the Alps, and of course, some of the churches and museums.

We spent our last evening together at the restaurant on the cliff above the Horse Pond at the end of Getriedegasse. The outdoor terraced levels look out on the Altstadt, and big searchlights highlight different landmarks.

The next morning, we escorted Bonnie and Wendy to the Bahnhof, they were off to Munchen. Bill and I would have gone with them, but we had already blown our whole stash on the dinner and drinks the night before. We took pictures of each other, and I took a picture of both of them from the platform while they stood inside their compartment with the window down waving good-bye to us. I keep this picture pasted to the inside of my wall locker, and I often think about my Canadian leave in Salzburg, Austria.

I found myself again in Salzburg, and I found a little happy there too, eh.

18

T. C. Q. C. AT GRAFENWÖHR

THESE TWO THINGS, T. C. Q. C. and Grafenwöhr, are entwined in a perpetual nightmare of bitter cold, the lingering scent of cordite and exhaust fumes, the recurrent waves of exploding ordnance, the staccato rattle of machine-gun fire, and the thrill of it all.

And, to put an even finer point on this time and place, the two most exhilarating things about wintertime in Grafenwöhr are, it is so hot in the shower tents that we can walk from our shower back to our squad tent buck naked and never even feel the bitter cold. The other thing is the pent up anxieties that come from the insistent pressures of the Tank Crew Qualification Course are always there lying in the grass waiting for someone to screw up.

We get up way too early, hurriedly hump and bust ammo in the dark, then [this might sound familiar] we sit around and freeze our asses off waiting for something to happen. The Range NCO walks off, and we break out the smokes, the jokes, and we pass around a canteen of Jägermeister schnapps to burn off the chill.

After a while, in the cold winter mist of the Oberpfalz, we hear them in the distance, the soft rhythmic whirling squeals, squeaks and clinks of road wheels turning. As they get closer and louder the hard rumbling vibrations of 52 ton tanks on the move shake the ground underneath us, and out of the shadows of the early morning haze, we see M Company's tanks crawl up the road to line up here at the Zero Range.

In the next little while, all of the 3d Reconnaissance Squadron's M60A1 tank crews will qualify on each of the twelve Tank Tables of T. C. Q. C. They will move from the Zero Range through the machine-gun and 20mm canon ranges, all the way up to and through Table VIII where the 105mm main gun is used in six daytime engagements and four nighttime engagements. All they have to do here is roll down range identify each and every target within seconds [enemy personnel, enemy tank, whether stationary or a moving target], acquire the target, and destroy the target, and accomplish all this in daylight or dark without being disqualified for killing any friendly targets which may be anywhere down range among the other targets.

Table VIII is what counts. Table VIII is the real test of the crews, and everything happens so fast there is really no time to think so, the cumulative effects of the hours and hours training kick in, and on the last run, in what seems like hours is over with in minutes and they have the score or they don't. If they do, the celebrations start, if they don't the grumbling and accusations soon recede into the preparations to do it all over again.

The training that makes all this possible doesn't even count the many thousands of hours of playing Army out there in the back alleys of America. And, if playing Army ever occupied even a moderate amount of your childhood, then this is the ultimate experience of the game in all its glory, and it's all done with live ammunition so, the sound effects are also real, along with the concussion of each shell exploding, and the flashes of light on the horizon.

Just about everything was going as well as could be expected, when the unthinkable happened. An M60A1, one of M Company's tanks, rolled off Table VIII with a perfect score. This is when the Tables turned on us, so to speak.

Everyone knows that if an enlisted man is to have a successful experience in the U. S. Army there is a certain protocol that must be followed. It goes something like this, well; actually, it goes exactly like this:

The Enlisted Man's Survival Protocol

Don't ever get in the front of a line, or the back of a line.

Don't ever get in the first rank or the last rank of a formation.

Don't volunteer for anything.

Don't ever let an Officer get to know your real name.

Don't look anyone in the eye, but don't look away either.

And, whatever you do, don't do anything to call attention to yourself.

It was just a foolish thing to do. No one, and I mean no one we ever heard of comin off Table VIII with a perfect score. From that very moment we knew that this was something just too dangerous to be around, and we were right

To make matters worse, there was a Stars & Stripes guy and a Stars & Stripes photographer out there on the range that day which made it a certainty that all the wrong people would hear about this, and we knew we were about to be overrun with all the wrong kind of attention.

In a panic, the X.O. scrambled around, rounded up about three hundred of us to shovel fresh snow all over the Field Motor Stables and all the walkways in between all the tents [so it would look pretty]. The C.O. organized an impromptu tank wash rack in the bitter cold next to the Motor Stables which promptly turned into a quaint little outdoor ice rink in about a half an hour. And, the Adjutant, who knows better than most, just encouraged everyone to clean up a little, slap some polish on our boots, and find a good place to hide.

They showed up in staff cars and helicopters, by train and by plane, and before long Grafenwöhr was crawling with brass from Seventh Army, VII Corps, Regiment, and even the local Bundeswehr Panzer commander showed up to congratulate the Top Tank Crew and all of these guys wanted to get their picture in the Stars & Stripes Newspaper. I think they must get points toward their next promotion for the number of times they make the front page of Stars & Stripes, or maybe they just wish they did.

Of course, this was a great accomplishment, and one that certainly should be recognized, but this kind of up close recognition always leads to some kind of a fly in the buttermilk reversal of fortune.

Recognizing the horrible mistake they had made, the Top Tank Crew couldn't even enjoy the cases of beer that were waiting for them, and they tried their best to keep the lowest profile possible to no avail. However, they graciously acknowledged the claps on the back and the commendations and all that, but always tried to slip into the background at every opportunity.

Surprisingly, outside of one USAREUR General with the customary distaste for actually eating a meal in a field mess tent, or the occasional lack of decorum in the ranks in response to these fumbling officers who insisted on getting in the way of the actual work, we were doing pretty well with our esteemed guests.

When most of the hooting and hollering was over with, and our brass laden guests were clearing out to go to their next road engagement, we thought we had it made and things were beginning to look pretty ordinary again, when it happened.

A Specialist Frank caught up with General D. G. Seeum in the head shed and informed him that his wife had arrived and was awaiting him in the General's staff car, which was parked just out beyond the mess tent.

At the same time, the gorgeous Mrs. D. G. Seeum got tired of waiting on D. G. and got out of the staff car and started walking up toward the head shed.

In the meantime, Billy Wayne, unaware there was any threat still lurking in the greater Grafenwöhr area was just finishing up his shower.

The General and Mrs. Seeum met up in mid camp just about the time Billy Wayne bounded out of the shower tent buck naked. There were seven of us who witnessed this whole thing, so I have corroboration, if anyone needs it.

Billy Wayne, even at Parade Rest, is one of the most well equipped troopers we have in the 2d Armored Cavalry, if not all of USAREUR. And, he didn't even break stride, he just looked up, gave the General the most casual ordinary hand salute ever rendered a general in the history of the U. S. Army, and as he bisected the merging path of the General and Mrs. Seeum he just went right on walking. While the General, unflustered by just another naked G.I. to our astonishment returned Billy Wayne's salute and kept on walking.

However, we watched Mrs. Seeum's mouth gape open, and while keeping all eyes on Billy, she walked head on into the General, bounced off him, and fell backwards into the snow.

M Company might have had a crew with the perfect score on Table VIII, and the Top Tank honors, but over at Headquarters Troop, we had the Top Gun at Grafenwöhr, our own Billy Wayne.

19

ON THE BORDER

THE REAL MISSION of the 2nd Armored Cavalry Regiment during our time here was to patrol our piece of the 731 km border between the west, West Germany [the Federal Republic of Germany] and the east, East Germany [the German Democratic Republic [East Germany], and Czechoslovakia], on a border euphemistically called, the Iron Curtain.

In the 3rd Reconnaissance Squadron, the real soldiers who actually did this were the recon troopers of I Troop, K Troop, L Troop, M Company, and the Howitzer Battery. They served on a rotating basis of thirty-day tours of duty at the border camps, Camp Röetz, and Camp Weiden, and other border camps.

The border is like another world, or another two worlds. On one side its mostly just rural countryside, and on the other side it's a fortress. The border is defined by watchtowers with interlocking fields of sight, mine fields, ditches dug that slope into a vertical wall to prevent anyone from crashing through the border from the east, electrified fences topped with concertina wire, automatic explosives embedded in the fences, patrolled by armed border guards, police dogs, listening posts, and mobile patrols. This is not an ordinary place, it's a terrifying barrier for the people on the wrong side of it, and it's our surreal image of what totalitarian tyranny actually looks like.

They watch us; we watch them.

Twenty-four hours a day, seven days a week, in all kinds of weather, our Recon Troops of each of the Reconnaissance Squadrons of the 2nd Armored Cavalry Regiment stands watch all along the 2nd Cav's portion of the Iron Curtain. In fact, a continuous unbroken line of American G.I.s stretching back from the chaos of post war Europe up to the time the Eastern Block nations dissolved into to their present day form of government, mostly free of the influence of Russia, we have always stood post on the Iron Curtain.

Equipped with ground surveillance radar, weapons locked and loaded, mobile patrols, listening posts, Observation Posts, M60A1 tanks, M109 Self Propelled Howitzers, conventional and tactical nuclear weapons, and air surveillance ongoing in an unending patrol of the borders of eastern Europe, we keep watch. And, each individual on post along this border knew that just across the way not far from this barrier, there were 250 divisions of the Warsaw Pact nations poised to respond to any incident, any order, any excuse, to make the Cold War into a hot one.

And, the most amazing thing is, all of these guys knew that all they were doing was being the ante up for the next conflict, and all they were supposed to do is attempt to hold the line long enough for the rest of the United States Armed Forces and the rest of world to react, and come to our aid.

Standing here, on our side, it feels a little weird, a little scary, and a whole lot like something terrible might happen, and sometimes it does. On patrol, or in the sack after a heavy snowfall, in the silence of the night, one or a dozen land mines will explode all at once under the weight of the snow, or under the careless step of a refugee. When someone makes an attempt at the wire, small arms fire might interrupt the silence. If the refugees are shot, sometimes they lie there for weeks. If they make it across, they kiss the ground, praise us for being here, release the burdens of their ordeal in tears and laughter and pain if they're wounded.

I don't know if we'll ever do anything as important as this in all our lives, all I know is I'm proud to say we were here, and I'm especially proud of the guys in the line troops, I Troop, K Troop, L Troop, M Company, and How Battery who did this every day and every night during all the years we watched and waited.

In the tense atmosphere following the Soviet invasion and occupation of Czechoslovakia in '68, the 3rd Reconnaissance Squadron remained on high alert for months.

With our personnel and equipment resources stretched to the limit, we began to show signs of the wear and tear in our significant effort to maintain a show of force and fulfill our NATO/USAREUR mission without any obvious cracks in our fortress of defense on our side of the Iron Curtain. These circumstances put us to the test, and in the best traditions of the United States Cavalry, we answered the call, and rode to the rescue.

Even Marty, our Courts and Boards clerk, volunteered to take his place on the wall, and went up to the Border near the Waidhaus crossing to walk a post on freedom's first line of defense. Actually, he was part of an I Troop three man mobile patrol driving a stretch of border reporting on Soviet troop movements.

On his third round of patrols, his I Troop jeep gave up just after his patrol's Prick 25 radio battery pack failed. One man stayed with the jeep, one went north, and Marty went south hoping to locate the relief patrol, or the O.D.

Fall in the Oberpfalz can be unusually cold after dark, or just chilly if you're lucky. Marty was lucky, and except for the fact he didn't know where he was, or what to do about it, he walked along watching the sun recede toward a western horizon.

When Marty crossed one of the abandoned roads that used to bisect the border of West Germany and Czechoslovakia, he heard the distinctive roar of a Soviet battle tank. Turning to look eastward, on a little rise just across the border he saw the low slung profile of the tank, it came to a stop, the red star on the turret bathed in sunlight. Marty stopped there, too, staring off into Czechoslovakia, and the Soviet tank's turret and cannon trained its 100mm barrel on the Courts and Boards clerk of the 3rd Reconnaissance Squadron, 2nd Armored Cavalry, but our Marty did not flinch. Well, actually, in an act of dignified defiance, he stood his ground, and quite emphatically shot them the finger, and hustled off out of sight.

You won't find this account in any of the annals of our Cold War victories, but to us Marty will always be our Cold War Hero.

20

ORGANIZATION DAYS

THE 2D ARMORED Cavalry Regiment is the oldest continuously organized unit in the United States Army. On 23 May 1836 the unit was organized as the 2d Dragoons. This distinction is the impetus for an annual event called, of all things, Organization Day. Organization Day is celebrated by a congregation of the four squadrons of the 2d Armored Cavalry and the Nurnberg Headquarters Group [about 5,500 of us, not counting civil servants and dependents and the assigned support units] in an all day extravaganza consisting of a review of the troops parade, athletic games, a picnic, free beer, and a speech by the Commanding Officer of the regiment.

To give you some idea of the dedication and passionate commitment of the troops of the 2d Armored Cavalry, I'd like to mention our motto. The motto of the 2d Armored Cavalry is, "Remember your regiment, follow your officers", the author of this motto was Brevet Major Ripley Arnold. Brevet Major Arnold was shot in the back by one of his own men. I have a special place in my heart for Major Arnold and for this organization as the 2d Dragoons founded my hometown, Fort Worth, Texas, and our Major Arnold is buried there.

In Germany, the 2d Armored Cavalry is stationed in Nurnberg, the regimental Headquarters at Merrell Barracks, the 1st Squadron is stationed in Bindlach at Christensen Barracks, and on the border at Camp Gates, the 2d Squadron is stationed in Bamberg, at Warner Barracks, and on the border at Camp Hof, we were stationed in Amberg on the Pond, and on the border at Camp Roetz, the 4th Squadron is the Aviation Squadron, we never knew where they were, exactly, or where they were going, except for the times when one or more of us gets MedEvacted to Nurnberg [ask anyone about going to see Major Flowers, M.D., but you have to see Specialist Flowers first [no relation]. Major Flowers, M.D. is the shrink for the 2d Armored Cavalry, Specialist Flowers is his assistant. If you ask nice, or just act goofy, you can get MedEvaced to Nurnberg to see Specialist Flowers and Specialist Flowers through the grace and benevolence of Major Flowers can get you a three day pass for a clandestine R & R. in Nurnberg if you really need it, or sometimes even if you don't'.

The Organization Day festivities were held in Nurnberg at the coliseum where the Nazis used to hold their huge rallies for Hitler. The place is made of white stone and concrete. You would immediately recognize this place because of that film clip they show all the time where the big huge iron Nazi swastika inside an iron laurel wreath mounted on the top of the stands is pictured. And in dramatic fashion this swastika gets blasted to pieces with explosives, and this is the place you see in all the old newsreels where Hitler is standing up there on the white stone platform haranguing his audiences. This is not a bad place for Organization Day, there's plenty of room for everything.

The first Organization Day that I remember participating in was the one on 23 May 1968 in Nurnberg. We put on our Class A uniforms, drew our weapons, and assembled in the Motor Stables where we climbed aboard deuce and halfs and 5 ton trucks to haul us up to this event. This was not exactly a good idea.

So, we dismounted at the coliseum, formed up, had our parade, listened to the C.O. talk about this place, our mission, our proud history, and finally the free beer, and we sat down to lunch. We watched some softball games, drank some more beer, we watched some track and field events, drank some more beer, we wandered around the coliseum, drank some more beer, we spit on the platform where Hitler stood, drank some more beer, we tried to find our jackets, hats, boots, and drank some more beer. Then, they yelled at us to go back to the parking area and get on the trucks.

We found T.J. in the parking lot, he was on a 2d Squadron truck headed for Bamberg, we found Jay on a 1st Squadron truck headed for Bindlach, we found Dave and Pete on a 4th Squadron helicopter headed for who knows where, but we finally managed to get everyone onto a 3d Squadron truck, but there was no driver.

Jacinto stood up in the back of our truck, looked around, and said, "Hey, ya'll look at dis." We stood up, looked across the parking area and laughed ourselves silly. On some trucks there were two or three people, other trucks were crammed with twenty-five to thirty people, guys were puking off the sides, none of the trucks could move because they had put up barricades around the parking lot, there was a bunch of hooting and hollering, all some guys had on were their boots and pants, if anyone had a hat on, it was on backwards, there were some German girls on dozens of trucks, and it was complete chaos all around.

After several long minutes of honking and hollering, Billy Wayne showed up and drove our truck right through the barricades and that started the flow of traffic out of the parking lots. No one remembers how long it took us to get back to Amberg, because Billy Wayne [our driver who has a heart of gold] kept stopping to pick up guys walking along the road. They were walking because their truck was in a ditch, broken down, or they put some guys off for puking on other people in the truck. The amazing thing was, no one was killed or injured, and except for a few trucks disabled by drunken drivers, this was the best fun we had for a very long time.

The following year, some creative genius at regiment decided to transport all of us to Nurnberg on the trains. This was not exactly a good idea, either.

So, when we got off the train at the Bahnhof, we formed up, marched over to the coliseum, and had our parade, listened to the C.O. talk about this place, our mission, our proud history, and finally the free beer, and we sat down to lunch. We watched some softball games, drank some more beer, we watched some track and field events, drank some more beer, we wandered around the coliseum, drank some more beer, and in keeping with tradition, we spit on the platform where Hitler stood, drank some more beer, we tried to find our jackets, hats, boots, and drank some more beer. Then, they yelled at us to go back to the Bahnhof, it was time to go.

When most everyone was back on the train, the first order of business was for some of the officers to go through the train compartments and roust out all the German girls, this took a long time.

Jay showed up shirtless with Olga who was topless; I don't think Olga was German. She sounded Hungarian or maybe Romanian, but she was beautiful. Some officer pulled our compartment door open and yelled at Olga. Olga started crying and Jay took a swing at the officer. What's so surprising is that I don't think Jay had ever hit anyone, but he made history with this punch, the officer went down like a bag of rocks, and we hustled Olga and Jay out of there. When the officer came to, he wanted names and ranks, but we told him we didn't know the crazy Hungarian pimp who hit him, but we pointed to the platform and told him he went that way.

On the train back to Amberg, there were two guys in some compartments and fifteen in others. After a while most everyone went to sleep, and when the train pulled up in Amberg and we got off it took a long time for this long strung out line of walking wounded to weave its way through town and climb up the hill back up to the Pond.

Almost all of us had to buy different pieces of our Class A uniforms we lost in the battles of Organization Day. The Morning Report the next day had a suspicious number of people on sick call, AWOL, or in civilian custody, but things were back to normal in a few days.

You have to like Organization Day, if not for the parade, the sporting events, there's always plenty of free beer, and you get to spit on the platform where Hitler stood.

21

S.T.A.G.G.

S.T.A.G.G. STANDS FOR SHORT TIMERS A GO GO, a kind of a milestone monitor of anticipatory rotation back to your old HOR [Home of Record] in the good old U.S.A. In the Ol' Personality Shoppe at the back hanging on the cabinet under the coffee pot is a colorful board with big letters at the top that read, S.T.A.G.G. and there is a grease pencil dangling from a string attached to the board.

The columns underneath the big S.T.A.G.G. letters are the name column and the days column. The name column holds the names of everyone in the Personality Shop, and the days column holds the number of days each of us has before we rotate back home for our release from active duty. The S.T.A.G.G. and the lines for the columns and the column descriptions are written in permanent marker on the board, and a heavy duty plastic covers the board, and the names of the people in the office, and the number of days they have are written in grease pencil on the plastic so they can be changed, the names every now and then, the numbers every day.

At the end of each day the person at the bottom of the board [the person with the most days left before rotation back to the world] erases all the numbers in the numbers column and reduces the number for each person by one, and writes the new number on the board next to each person's name. This calculation is further complicated by the method we use to calculate the number of days we have left. The calculation is considered correct when the number of days posted is the number of days that we have left minus one day because in fine print under the last name and number on the bottom of the board there is the qualification that reads, "And a wake-up", meaning there is actually one additional day that is not posted on the board, this particular day is the day you leave so you don't want to count it, because the day you leave is really not a full day, and it makes the number of days you have to go look like there are less days than there really are, don't cha see.

When someone first gets to their assignment in Germany this seems like a crazy way to make the whole thing drag out, and it makes it seem like the time passes ever more excruciatingly slower each day. But, as the time goes by, and the connection to these people and this place gets more and more familiar then something happens to your insides when you begin to realize that the day is coming when you are going to have to leave your friends here and go home, which by the time it is your time to go is not such a sweet deal because these are your friends, and after you leave your friends here will still be here having fun, without you, which is a real unsettling thing that you cannot necessarily change except by the suicidal act of re-enlisting and no one, no matter how much they love these guys is going to do such a thing. So, what we end up with after all this time, this attention to detail, this marking of time, is we know exactly when we are going to leave the best friends we've ever had, and go home, which now seems not so much like a place we necessarily want to be if these people here are not going to be there, too.

There is no way to really change this, so what we have to do is really get into it. This means we make a big deal out of each little milestone it takes us to climb up the board to the top, where we all disappear. These stages include things like the day you become a 90 Day Loss.

A 90 Day Loss is a person who has, you guessed it, 90 days or less before rotation back to the States. This means that somewhere in the grand scheme of things, there is some clerk deep down in the dark recesses of Headquarters of the Department of the Army in Washington D.C. that gets your name sent to him so he can go requisition another you to fill your slot on the T. O. & E. of the United States Army Europe, so in the grand scheme of maintaining about 250,000 G.I.s in a obligatory bound agreement called the N.A.T.O. treaty things will remain static.

This is probably the only time in your life when your inter-galactic global international number comes up, and someone has to do something about it.

Nevertheless, it does not mean you should attach any importance to this event even though your ego might try to go this way.

So, some clerk in training somewhere in the USA, or some 90 Day Loss in some other unit in the United States Army is tapped on the shoulder and given orders to report to the Pond to replace you in the 3d Reconnaissance Squadron here in Amberg, so you can go home, which is a pretty amazing thing given all the little cogs and wheels in this gigantic machine called the United States Army.

Of course, when you become a 90 Day Loss your status automatically rises among the ranks, and everyone kind of gives you a nod of respect or a giggle, if they are also a 90 Day Loss, as they pass you in the hallways. This status also leads to a whole new language of shortness, which gets as creative as the person who is so short he can feel it. Like, "I'm not short, I'm next!" for those who have really almost made the whole trip. And, even the ones who have a little time left who can't help themselves join in, "I'm so short, I don't have to shine my boots again." or "I'm so short, if I fall asleep I might miss my train," or "I'm so short, my girlfriend dumped her new boyfriend," or "I'm so short, I'm giving away my ration card," or 'I'm so short, I can write myself a letter and get home to read it when it gets there," or "I'm so short, I don't have to break starch again," and on and on ad nauseam.

Somewhere about this time, you have to think about Clearing Post. Clearing Post means you go around and let everyone know your leaving and turn in stuff you don't need anymore, pay your bar bill at the EM or NCO Clubs, give away your extra stuff you won't need [like most of the 33 pairs of socks and underwear you bought so you would only have to wash your clothes every thirty days], say goodbye to your German and refugee friends, girlfriends, and drinking buddies downtown, kiss the Buschbohm Sisters goodbye, and return the stuff you've borrowed.

The first order of business in this process is getting a Short Timers clipboard and a Short Timers Stick [aka a Swagger Stick], a Short Timers Stick is a little riding crop [a cavalry thing] you carry under your arm as you swagger around the Pond clearing post.

The first hurdle in clearing post is getting around Svetlana. Svetlana is the pretty blond Ukrainian refugee girl who is always hanging around looking to marry a G.I. and go to Amerika. You have to be very careful with Svetlana. There is nothing Svetlana wouldn't do to get her ticket stateside, and therefore there is nothing you shouldn't do to keep from getting married to Svetlana. Most everyone was able to do this, that is, everyone except Billy Wayne. Svetlana got Billy Wayne to marry her. She thought she had it made, then Billy Wayne took a European discharge and went to work for the Army & Air Force Exchange Service [AAFES] here in Germany. So, Svetlana may have gotten her G.I. but she is still here with us and Billy Wayne.

The rest is easy. You may have to borrow a couple of glove liners, maybe a pile cap in order to get S-4 to clear you [before you leave you have to turn in all your cold weather gear [your TA 50-901] but this is about the worst of it. The only thing is if you're the last guy here you may be paying for a few hundred dollars for lost cold weather gear that you never had in the first place, or you loaned out to people who did, but now they're gone.

When all this is said and done, the day finally comes to go home. This is a very emotional day. If Eddy were still here, he would play ['Aloha Oe', the Hawaiian farewell song, for you on the piano in the USO Club].

There will be a little ceremony in the Personality Shop; you get to break your swagger stick over your knee. Then, you get your picture made holding the S.T.A.G.G. board, pointing at your name and number with your crooked swagger stick with a big Zero where your number of days left should be. Then, without taking off your Raincoat you say good bye to everyone, and some of the guys take you down to the Bahnhof, drink a few beers with you, everyone signs your beer coaster and walks you up to the platform, and you get on board, look out the window, and wave farewell to a little group of folks standing on the platform, sometimes even some of the Germans come down to bid you a fond farewell. Then, the train pulls out of town, and you sit down and think about what an amazing experience it was, and what a great bunch of guys you're leaving behind, and how you'll never forget all this, how it's actually kind of sad to be leaving, and how you'll always have a place in your heart for this time, this place, and these people, and this extraordinary experience.

Epilogue

From 1945 until 1992 thousands and thousands of American G.I.s spent a small piece of their youth on the Pond in Amberg, Germany and all over USAREUR. At our age, this place and time shaped much of our understanding of life, the essence of friendship, the concept of duty, the legacy of our fathers, and a renewed appreciation for the place we called home.

To our great benefit our service here brought together a group of people who made a long lasting and permanent impression in all of our lives from this point forward. And, although we may not have realized it until we stuck our head out the window of the train taking us away, we knew it then, and we know it now, no matter what happens to us, all these guys & gals will be part of us forever, even those who may have left this world before us, they will never leave our best memories of them. And, I know we're bound to see them again when we all get to Fiddler's Green.

IMMER GERADEAUS!